FAITH OF OUR

FATHERS,

LIVING STILL

A Study Guide for the
Five Points of Calvinism

Paul H. Treick

Modesto, California
2014

Library of Congress
Catalog Card No. 97-68652

ISBN No. 13:97-1495430503

First Printing, March 1992
Second Printing, April 1993
Third Printing, June 1997
Revised Fourth Printing, 2014

The Scriptures, unless otherwise noted, are from the New King James Bible.

Dedicated with gratitude to my father

and my forefathers, who by God's grace

kept the faith entrusted to them

by their Heavenly Father,

with the hope that this precious faith

may always be alive in the

hearts and minds of their children.

TABLE OF CONTENTS

PREFACE

"Faith of our fathers, living still
in spite of dungeon, fire and sword;
O how our hearts beat high with joy
whene'er we hear God's glorious Word;
Faith of our fathers, holy faith!
We will be true to thee till death. "
(Frederick W. Faber, 1849)

The *faith of our fathers* is a faith which has been seriously eroding in recent years. In the Reformed Church we hold it precious, not for the sake of tradition, but because that faith was one which our Heavenly Father entrusted to us and our children, as the basis of His Covenant of Grace, that we might know His saving grace in Jesus Christ. May we, by God's help, be faithful and true to the glorious doctrines of His grace as He has revealed them to us in His Holy Word.

How the Psalmist also yearned for this: *"I will open my mouth in a parable: I will utter dark sayings of old: Which we have heard and known, and our fathers have told us. We will not hide them from their children, showing to the generation to come the praises of the LORD, and his strength, and his wonderful works that he hath done. That the generation to come might know them, even the children which should be born; who should arise and declare them to their children. "* (Ps. 78:2-4,6)

In speaking of our "fathers," we think historically first of the Patriarchs – Abraham, Isaac, and Jacob; then of Moses, David, and the prophets of God; then of the apostles such as Peter, John, and Paul; then of the Reformers of the sixteenth century, especially John Calvin;

and finally of our own covenant fathers and grandfathers, many of whom have given of themselves that these precious truths of Scripture should still live in the hearts of their children.

Therefore, this study is directed to covenant parents and to their children, that together they might joyfully confess that this faith is *"living still"* in their hearts and lives.

God Is Sovereign By Nature

A correct understanding of and a belief in the doctrine of the *sovereignty of God* is an absolute essential to the Christian faith. This doctrine is not optional for Christians, nor are any of the doctrines that flow from it. God's absolute right, power, and authority constitute the core of every teaching concerning the Christian's faith and life.

The doctrine of God's absolute sovereignty constitutes the nucleus of the Reformed faith. Yet it is not a "Reformed" doctrine which some theologians have simply concocted and preserved through history. It is the teaching of the Holy Scriptures which each and every Christian is called upon to confess. Only with this foundation can "God be God."

There remains, not only among the critics of the Reformed Faith, but even among some who claim to adhere to the Reformed faith, a serious misunderstanding, misinterpretation, and misapplication of the doctrine of God's sovereignty, and especially so in the area of "salvation by grace." This is certainly not due to the lack of perspicuity in the Scripture. It is most likely due to a lack of study of Scripture or, even more alarming, to a deliberate and sinful attempt to resist God's sovereignty in favor of human autonomy (where man is a law unto himself).

While God is the sovereign ruler over all of our life (in areas of creation, providence, history, science, etc.), this study is confined to the matter of His sovereign grace in the salvation of man. This teaching is the basis for many statements of faith such as the *Heidelberg Catechism*, *The Belgic Confession of Faith*, and the *Westminster Confession of Faith*, and it is difficult to find any better summary of this teaching than in the creed known as the *Canons of Dort*.

The Five Points of Calvinism

The *Canons of Dort* present to us five major doctrines concerning our salvation. They are more popularly known to us as the *"Five Points of Calvinism,"* not because John Calvin (1509-1564) wrote them, (since he was already with the Lord when the Synod of Dort met in 1618), but because Calvin, among many other Reformers, had previously reopened the eyes of the Church to this teaching of the Scriptures. The doctrines of grace formulated were not the inventions of Calvin, but are the teachings of Scripture which Calvin and others have carefully examined and systematically outlined. God forbid we should ever build our faith on the teachings or authority of any mere man or manmade creed. The Five Points of Calvinism are not historically conditioned doctrines which eventually can be abandoned, but they are the teachings of our Sovereign, Covenant God. Christians for generations have given life and possessions that these truths may be upheld.

At the mention of "Calvinism" many mouths drop open – aghast that anyone still believes in these antiquated teachings anymore. Such reaction usually indicates two things – a lack of knowledge of what Calvin actually taught and, more seriously, an ignorance of Scripture. My effort in this short study is to demonstrate from Scripture that God is sovereign just as Calvin and multitudes of people since then have taught and believed.

For the most part "Calvinism" is falsely characterized by opponents to the doctrines of grace. It is necessary to counter such portrayals and to present these doctrines from the perspective of someone who actually believes these teachings.

Arminianism

The most outspoken archrival of the doctrine of God's sovereignty is a system of doctrine which has come to be known as *"Aminianism."* Arminianism cannot stand the test of Scripture and must therefore be considered an egregious error which depends on sinful man's concept of human justice and freedom. The fires of Arminianism which have burned their way into the majority of church denominations were fanned by such movements in history as the

Renaissance, the French Enlightenment, Revivalism, Liberalism, Neo-Evangelicalism, and today's Post Modern Self-Esteem Theology.

Arminianism continues yet today as an attempt to exalt man, the natural result of which is to dethrone God. Not only the absolute power of God, but the authority (*ie.* His right) and justice of God are called into question and denied. If God is no longer the sovereign God revealed to us in Scripture, then Satan has succeeded in his deception first taught to Adam and Eve, *"you will be like God, knowing good and evil."* (Gen. 3:5 NKJV) Arminianism is certainly not a new concept. It had its roots in the Fall; the result of which was that man desired "autonomy" in which he claimed the right to make all his own choices according to his own will which he admits is slightly tarnished, yet still retains the ability to make good choices. This proud spirit is evident in those who reject God's perfect, sovereign will over them.

In fairness to many who espouse Arminian doctrines, it should be noted that few of them have ever been exposed to the real teachings of Calvinism. Some detractors have never thought through their own faith sufficiently to see its real ramifications and logical conclusions.

A Present Concern

I am concerned with the state of the Christian Church today. It may appear to some to be undergoing a healthy numerical expansion. Yet, I fear that it is being built with shoddy and combustible materials (*cf.* I Cor. 3:11-15). The confessions of Christians have been reduced to "I believe in Jesus." According to Acts 16:31, that is the requirement for salvation and we rejoice to hear those words. But sadly, that confession often has little definition. Who is the *I*? What is *belief*? Where does it come from? How long will it last? Who is *Jesus*? Why was He sent? For whom did He die? For whose glory am I saved? How do you explain the unbelief of many who hear and reject the gospel? How is it that I have come to believe? Will this faith, and hence my salvation, last, and if so, by whose power?

It is appalling to witness the number of people in Reformed Churches who are really "closet Arminians." They can neither define nor defend the Scripture's teaching on the sovereignty of God in all things. For some, this is an optional doctrine. Many consistently fail to see the distinction between the Creator and the creature. Some appear to actually apologize for the Reformed faith, as though it did not come from the Word of God. While many claim to be in the Calvinistic tradition historically, they betray themselves by their own confessions and lives.

An increasing number of people consider matters of doctrine to be nothing more than the egalitarian opinions of one ecclesiastical body to be on an equal par with the opinions of another. Furthermore, they liberally declare that everyone is entitled to their personal opinions.

God does not offer us mere opinions in the matter of salvation. He is not the Author of confusion, but of truth. He does not teach two opposing pathways to life. God nowhere reveals His sovereignty as an optional belief. Nor does He offer a series of multiple theological choices – where the correct answer is "all of the above." The Bible reveals who man is and who God is. It does not leave this matter open to the speculations and formulations of depraved man.

Those who respond by saying, "But Arminianism works too" are woefully ignorant of God's concept of Truth. Have we now reached the point of adopting a Machiavellian approach to theology, where the "end justifies the means"? The "end" (as well as the "beginning") of all things must be the glory of God, not human claims to success.

And, what about this "end?" I have encountered enough Arminians who have no actual, solid, enduring comfort in their faith. They remain unsure as to their end. It is simply impossible for any man-centered theology to produce real comfort and peace to the soul. Yet, let's be clear on this – whether Arminianism or Calvinism, "what works" is not the issue. The only valid consideration is whether it is *true*.

The doctrine of God's sovereignty is the teaching of the Bible. It is the heart of the gospel. It ought to be sweeping the world instead of being brushed aside as a relic of an outdated system of doctrine. We need Christians with the courage and zeal to say, as Martin Luther did many years ago regarding the Bible, "Here I stand. I can do no other."

My purpose in examining the subject of the *sovereignty of God and His grace* is not simply to win some theological debate, but to provide answers and clarification to this doctrine. It is not my intention to condemn Arminians, but to correct some serious errors they hold, and this, for their benefit. It is impossible to treat this subject without reference to Arminianism since the formulation of the Five Points of Calvinism grew out of the Remonstrant challenge.

We also need to set the record straight on the often misunderstood teaching of what is known as "Calvinism." We adhere to the teaching of the Bible, and to what Calvin taught insofar as it is in agreement with the Bible. Only if our salvation is properly understood can all the glory rightly be attributed to God alone. Only if we properly understand our own salvation can we spread the good news to others. Only if we build our faith on this solid foundation can we as Christians have real and lasting joy, comfort, and thanksgiving in our salvation. And, only if our salvation is rightly understood will we properly give all the praise and glory to God for it.

I am concerned that we maintain the correct starting point in the study of our salvation. If we fail at the outset, we will undoubtedly fail at every point along the way. If man begins with a false premise, he can only end up with a false result. Calvinism is a "system" of doctrine which is intricately woven together by Scripture. It is not a potshot approach where each doctrine is defined independently of others.

I hope to lay before the reader, as clearly as possible, the teaching of Scripture, with the hope that he will build his faith on this foundation. Those who continue in their determination to reject these doctrines will have to deal with them from the Bible, not from their opinion of what the Reformed Church believes and teaches. Ultimately this study should help us to be able to clearly answer the question, "What does it mean to say we are Reformed?"

My objective is to deal with a limited area of theology which I am convinced is most important for Christians – the doctrine of salvation, or "soteriology." I will be examining these under the five doctrinal headings called the "Five Points of Calvinism."

I am not inferring that "Calvinism" is limited to only five doctrines. There are some who claim they are "Calvinists" solely because they believe in the doctrines of grace, while rejecting Calvin's teaching regarding the covenant, sacraments, ecclesiology, and eschatology. Nor should we conclude that God reveals His "grace" only in soteriology. The Christian's entire faith and life is permeated with the grace and love of God. We are partakers of the Covenant of Grace. The glorious result of true faith is that we understand our release from the bondage of sin and our restoration to God's created purpose – that man is to bring glory to God in every moment and facet of his life, now and everlastingly.

Many excellent books have been written on this subject and I am indebted to their authors. I do not intend to expand on them, but to glean from them in order to briefly present in a workbook format the essential arguments and scriptural data necessary to a basic understanding which may spur your appetite for further study. I urge readers to use their Bibles and to faithfully look up the passages referred to. Furthermore, I encourage you to grapple with the questions and write down your answers which will help you retain them.

For further reading, I encourage you to read the books listed in the bibliography at the end of this study. The Scripture quoted will be from the New King James Version unless otherwise noted.

In conclusion, it is my hope and prayer that God will use this study to accomplish three things. First, may it edify and provide structure and deeper meaning to your faith. Secondly, that believing, you may lift your voice in praise to the sovereign, triune God for the gracious gift of salvation. And thirdly, that this study will equip you and fill you with a renewed zeal to proclaim this gospel of our sovereign God to others.

Paul H. Treick

Modesto, California
1992; revised, 2014

1

The Sovereignty of God

Before we can actually begin to examine the "Five Points of Calvinism" we must take the time to define what is meant by the *"sovereignty of God."* It will do little good to set forth the doctrines of salvation unless we have this foundational knowledge of who God is.

The sovereignty of God is not just one of many attributes of God, but it is the underlying nature of God which is the foundation for every teaching about who God is or what He has done. It is not an exaggeration to say that the feebleness of so much theology today is due to a lack of knowledge and faith in the sovereignty of our God.

Sovereignty defined

"Sovereignty" can be defined as the nature of God by which He exercises *absolute might and right* in ruling over all things according to His own good pleasure. He is in total control of all creation from eternity. God has not only the right to decree something, but the power to carry out His will precisely as He has determined. The most concise way of defining sovereignty, if properly understood, is to say that "God is God." Sovereignty is more than simply one aspect of the nature of God. If God is God, He is Sovereign! He can be nothing less. To reduce God's right or power even in the smallest degree is to create another god.

The very nature of God revealed in Scripture leaves no doubt as to His sovereign majesty. When, in the Second Commandment, God tells us that He is a *"jealous God,"* He is revealing His sovereignty (see Ex. 34:14). He alone has the right to demand that all praise, worship, and glory be afforded to Him and to no other.

Many Christians appear to reduce the meaning and extent of God's sovereignty to His reign over the natural world alone. If God is sovereign, then by definition, it is an *unlimited or absolute sovereignty* over all things – including the matter of salvation. It is important for our study to see clearly that *God's love, grace, and mercy are also sovereignly administered to whom, when, and how He wills.*

In Hebrew there is not a word that can exactly equal the word *"sovereign"* in our English language. However, where the words *"Jehovah adoni"* (Lord) occur, the New International Version (NIV) of the Bible translates this as *"Sovereign Lord"* which is probably the closest to the intent of the writer. The word *"Jehovah"* (or *"Yahweh"*) is usually translated *"LORD"* (all capital letters). The word *"Adoni"* is the word for *"Lord"* (small letters). However when both are used together (*ie.* *"Jehovah Adoni"*) it would be awkward to translate it *"LORD Lord,"* so the word *"Adoni"* was rendered as *"sovereign."* See Gen. 15:2; II Sam. 7:18; Ps. 71:16; Is. 25:8; 40:10; 50:4; 61:1,11; Jer. 32:17; Ezek. 12:28; Dan. 4:25 in the NIV translation.

In the New Testament Greek, the word that comes closest to the word *"sovereign"* is the word *"despotes"* (from which we have our English word "despot"). When that word occurs with the word *"kurios"* (*"Lord"*) the translators of the NIV have rendered these two words as *"sovereign Lord"* which is the intent in the two passages where these words occur (II Pet. 2:1; Jude 4).

The Eternal Nature of God

The study of the sovereignty of God must begin with His *eternity.* He has neither beginning nor end. When the Bible speaks about God as being *"everlasting"* or *"from everlasting"* (esp. in the KJV), it refers to His being without beginning or end and can best be translated as *"eternal"* (since, technically, "everlasting" has a beginning but has no end). Notice how this is taught in the passages below:

Rev. 1:8 *"I am the Alpha and the Omega, the Beginning and the End, says the Lord, who is and who was and who is to come, the*

Almighty."

Deut. 33:27 *"The eternal God is your refuge, and underneath are the everlasting arms; He will thrust out the enemy from before you, and will say, Destroy!"*

Ps. 41:13 *"Blessed be the LORD God of Israel From everlasting to everlasting! Amen and Amen."*

Ps. 102:12 *"But You, O LORD, shall endure forever, And the remembrance of Your name to all generations."*

Ps. 102:24-27 *"I said, O my God, Do not take me away in the midst of my days; Your years are throughout all generations. Of old You laid the foundation of the earth, And the heavens are the work of Your hands. They will perish, but You will endure; Yes, all of them will grow old like a garment; Like a cloak You will change them, And they will be changed. But You are the same, And Your years will have no end."*

Is. 43:13 *"Indeed before the day was, I am He; and there is no one who can deliver out of My hand; I work, and who will reverse it?"*

Is. 44:6 *"Thus says the LORD, the King of Israel, and his Redeemer, the LORD of hosts: I am the First and I am the Last; besides Me there is no God."* (see also Is. 48:12; Rev. 1:11)

God is the Creator

God is sovereign over all creation, because He is the *Creator of all things out of nothing.* A Creator is not only Almighty, but has the authority, right, and freedom to plan, create, and employ His creation in any manner that He wishes. God, as Creator, will govern all things only in a way that is consistent with His divine perfection and holiness. Scripture clearly reveals this as seen in the passages below:

Gen. 1:1 *"In the beginning God created the heavens and the earth."*

Is. 45:7,12,18 *"I form the light and create darkness, I make peace and create calamity; I, the LORD, do all these things. I have made the earth, and created man on it. It was I – My hands that stretched out the heavens, and all their host I have commanded. For thus says the LORD, Who created the heavens, Who is God, Who formed the earth and made it, Who has established it, Who did not create it in vain, Who formed it to be inhabited: I am the LORD, and there is no other."*

Heb. 11:3 *"By faith we understand that the worlds were framed by the word of God, so that the things which are seen were not made of things which are visible."*

Rev. 4:11 *"You are worthy, O Lord, to receive glory and honor and power; for You created all things, and by Your will they exist and were created."*

God is Self-Sufficient

Being the eternal Creator, God is *self-sufficient* – not dependent upon any creature either for His existence or for help to carry out His decrees. God states this most clearly when he calls His name "I AM WHO I AM. And He said, Thus you shall say to the children of Israel, I AM has sent me to you." (Ex. 3:14). Notice also the following passages:

Psa. 50:10-12 *"For every beast of the forest is Mine, and the cattle on a thousand hills. I know all the birds of the mountains, and the wild beasts of the field are Mine. If I were hungry, I would not tell you; For the world is Mine, and all its fullness."*

Jn. 5:26 *"For as the Father has life in Himself, so He has granted the Son to have life in Himself."*

Acts 17:24-25 *"God, who made the world and everything in it, since He is Lord of heaven and earth, does not dwell in temples made with hands. Nor is He worshiped with men's hands, as though He needed anything, since He gives to all life, breath, and all things."*

God makes it abundantly clear to Job in the closing chapters of the book of Job that He alone is sovereign. *No man may question the right of God to do as He pleases,* since it is God alone who has created and who preserves His creation. For anyone who still questions the right of God to do all things as He pleases, Job chapters 38-42 is "must" reading.

Job 38:2-4 *"Who is this who darkens counsel by words without knowledge? Now prepare yourself like a man; I will question you, and you shall answer Me. Where were you when I laid the foundations of the earth? Tell Me, if you have understanding."* So the Lord continues to flood Job with questions which he cannot answer – which only a sovereign Creator could answer.

Job 40:1-5 *"Moreover the LORD answered Job, and said: Shall the one who contends with the Almighty correct Him? He who rebukes God, let him answer it. Then Job answered the LORD and said: Behold, I am vile; what shall I answer You? I lay my hand over my mouth. Once I have spoken, but I will not answer; yes, twice, but I will proceed no further."*

Then finally, in Job 42:1-3, Job must humbly acknowledge that God alone is sovereign: *"Then Job answered the LORD and said: I know that You can do everything, and that no purpose of Yours can be withheld from You. You asked, Who is this who hides counsel without knowledge? Therefore I have uttered what I did not understand, things too wonderful for me, which I did not know."*

All Creatures are Dependent on God

While God is not dependent on any other being, man, on the other hand, is totally dependent on a sovereign God. This total dependence is an inseparable part of our nature as a *creature*. Our whole being and well-being is at the mercy of the good pleasure of God. *"For in him we live, and move, and have our being...."* (Acts 17:28) This is definitely not an undesirable or uncertain state to be in because believers are also the children of God who can expect only good things from their heavenly Father.

Notice what the Bible has to say to us about the sovereign care of our God:

I Sam. 2:6-8 *"The LORD kills and makes alive; He brings down to the grave and brings up. The LORD makes poor and makes rich; He brings low and lifts up. He raises the poor from the dust and lifts the beggar from the ash heap, to set them among princes and make them inherit the throne of glory. For the pillars of the earth are the Lord's, and He has set the world upon them."*

I Chron. 29:11-12 *"Yours, O LORD, is the greatness, the power and the glory, the victory and the majesty; for all that is in heaven and in earth is Yours; Yours is the kingdom, O LORD, and You are exalted as head over all. Both riches and honor come from You, and You reign over all. In Your hand is power and might; in Your hand it is to make great and to give strength to all."*

Eccl. 9:1 *"For I considered all this in my heart, so that I could declare it all: that the righteous and the wise and their works are in the hand of God. People know neither love nor hatred by anything that is before them."*

Ps. 145:15-19 *"The eyes of all look expectantly to You, And You give them their food in due season. You open Your hand And satisfy the desire of every living thing. The LORD is righteous in all His ways, Gracious in all His works. The LORD is near to all who call upon Him, To all who call upon Him in truth. He will fulfill the desire of those who fear Him; He also will hear their cry and save them."*

Is. 64:8 *"But now, O LORD, You are our Father; we are the clay, and You our potter; and all we are the work of Your hand."*

It has become a common error to see God's hand in the *"good"* things that happen to us, but to deny that God brings about *adversity* or suffering in our lives.

This error is the inevitable result of denying God His right to rule sovereignly. While it is true that Satan tempts man (*eg.* Adam and Job), he can do this only with the purpose and limitations which God determines. Satan may often be used by God to *try or test* the faith of man (see James 1:12-15). But, do not forget that it is always God who is in complete control.

It is common to hear a denial of God's sovereignty as demonstrated in His *providential* acts. The *Heidelberg Catechism* defines God's providence and its benefits in Questions 27 and 28. To intimate that some other power (such as the Devil) has the inherent freedom, power, or right to bring about anything independent of God is to deny the sovereign power of God. Yet, it is that denial that is expressed so often in the erroneous teaching that God is frustrated by all the forces working against Him. He is said to have a plan, but cannot carry it out because of the work of the Devil or man's stubbornness. That sort of limitation of God is a denial of the teaching of Scripture which declares that He performs all *things "according to His good pleasure"* and *"after the counsel of his own will"* (Eph. 1:5,9,11). Notice what the Bible says about this:

Job. 2:10 *"Shall we indeed accept good from God, and shall we not accept adversity? In all this Job did not sin with his lips."*

Prov. 16:4 *"The LORD has made all things for Himself, Yes, even the wicked for the day of doom."*

Is. 45:7b *"I make peace and create calamity; I, the LORD, do all these things."*

Rom. 9:15, 18 *"For He says to Moses, I will have mercy on whomever I will have mercy, and I will have compassion on whomever I will have compassion. Therefore He has mercy on whom He wills, and whom He wills He hardens."*

II Thess. 2:11, 12 *"And for this reason God will send them strong delusion, that they should believe the lie, that they all may be condemned who did not believe the truth but had pleasure in unrighteousness."*

If God is truly sovereign, then man certainly has no right to question the propriety of any act of God. *"But indeed, O man, who are you to reply against God? Will the thing formed say to him who formed it, Why have you made me like this? Does not the potter have power over the clay, from the same lump to make one vessel for honor and another for dishonor?"* (Rom. 9:20-21)

Certainly the once-humbled Nebuchadnezzar realized this about the God of Daniel when he said, *"And at the end of the time I, Nebuchadnezzar, lifted my eyes to heaven, and my understanding returned to me; and I blessed the Most High and praised and honored Him who lives forever: For His dominion is an everlasting dominion, and His kingdom is from generation to generation. All the inhabitants of the earth are reputed as nothing; He does according to His will in the army of heaven and among the inhabitants of the earth. no one can restrain His hand or say to Him, What have You done?"* (Dan. 4:34-

35)

Again, the Psalmist says, *"But our God is in heaven; He does whatever He pleases."* (Ps. 115:3)

God's Power is Absolute

The Omnipotent God carries out His plan in absolute sovereign power. We have become unaccustomed to the term "absolute" since "relativism" is the philosophy of our age. But Isaiah says, *"The LORD of hosts has sworn, saying, Surely, as I have thought, so it shall come to pass, and as I have purposed, so it shall stand: This is the purpose that is purposed against the whole earth, and this is the hand that is stretched out over all the nations. For the LORD of hosts has purposed, and who will annul it? His hand is stretched out, and who will turn it back?"* (Is. 14:24, 26, 27)

Again Isaiah says, *"Remember the former things of old, for I am God, and there is no other; I am God, and there is none like Me, declaring the end from the beginning, and from ancient times things that are not yet done, saying, My counsel shall stand, and I will do all My pleasure, calling a bird of prey from the east, the man who executes My counsel, from a far country. Indeed I have spoken it; I will also bring it to pass. I have purposed it; I will also do it."* (Is. 46:9-11)

Our Lord God is in absolute control of all things in order that His entire creation, which was created purely for His own glory, may fulfill this purpose. I Timothy 6:15, 16 describes God as *"the blessed and only Potentate, the King of kings and Lord of lords, who alone has immortality, dwelling in unapproachable light, whom no man has seen or can see, to whom be honor and everlasting power. Amen."*

God's Reign is Glorious

It is evident from Psalm 104 that the whole creation not only exists by God's gracious provisions, but it exists for His purposes and glory. *"May the glory of the LORD endure forever; May the LORD rejoice in His works."* (Ps. 104:31)

Romans 11:36 says, *"For of Him and through Him and to Him are all things, to whom be glory forever. Amen."* See also Ps.

119:89-91.

If God is the sovereign, eternal Creator who is able to perfectly perform all His holy will, then it follows that all things bring glory to God. Romans 9:22 and 23 speak of the *"vessels of his wrath prepared for destruction"* (*cf.* Rev. 15:1,7; 16:1) as well as *"the vessels of mercy, which He had prepared beforehand for glory."*

It must also follow that everything that man does – every facet of his existence – is likewise under the sovereign Lordship of God and must be performed for His glory. There are *no neutral areas* – no grey areas – which are sometimes referred to as "secular" or "natural."

All existence is by the supernatural power of God and conformable to His eternal decrees. So in man's existence, nothing comes about by chance. No part of the creation is "out of control" or left to the mercy of natural laws or to the whims of man or the Devil.

God's Sovereign Love, Mercy, and Grace

If man is *loved*, it is because God initiated this by His sovereign decree. God loves those whom He chooses to love (Eph. 1:4,5). It is not because man was so inherently loving or loveable, but simply because God sovereignly choose to love some and save them. *"In this is love, not that we loved God, but that He loved us."* and, *"We love him because He first loved us."* (I Jn. 4:10,19)

Paul recognizes the unconditional character of God's love when he says, *"Or who has first given to Him and it shall be repaid to him?"* (Rom. 11:35)

God's *mercy* to man is likewise sovereignly given to whomsoever He wills. Romans 9:15,16 teaches, *"For He says to Moses, I will have mercy on whomever I will have mercy, and I will have compassion on whomever I will have compassion. So then it is not of him who wills, nor of him who runs, but of God who shows mercy."*

And certainly God is sovereign in manifesting His *grace* to men. By it's very nature, "grace" is undeserved favor-- a free gift to enemies. No man can claim the *right* to grace. Similarly, no man has the right to demand a gift. A gift is not a payment for some good rendered, but, by its very nature, is freely given out of love. What sinful arrogance is expressed if we receive a gift and later claim that we received it due to our own efforts or that we were worthy of it because of some inherent good in us. That attitude destroys the very nature of a "gift" and of "grace." The Apostle Paul says, *"And if by grace, then it is no longer of works; otherwise grace is no longer grace. But if it is of works, it is no longer grace; otherwise work is no longer work."* (Rom. 11:6) Paul is careful to show the gracious nature of saving faith when he says in Eph. 2:8,9 *"For by grace you have been saved through faith, and that not of yourselves; it is the gift of God, not of works, lest anyone should boast."*

Certainly fallen man does not have the right (much less the ability or desire!) to claim salvation as his prerogative or entitlement. Man is justly under the curse of God. *"For when we were still without strength, in due time Christ died for the ungodly. For scarcely for a righteous man will one die; yet perhaps for a good man someone would even dare to die. But God demonstrates His own love toward us, in that while we were still sinners, Christ died for us."* (Rom. 5:6-8 NIV)

Every page of Scripture is replete with the teaching that God is a "sovereign" God. Each person of the Trinity exercises this sovereignty. If this very essential aspect of God's nature is removed, then He ceases to be the God of the Scriptures.

To Deny God's Sovereignty is Idolatry

Any denial of the sovereignty of God, whether in salvation or in providence, is an idolatrous denial of God and a violation of the First Commandment. If God does not perform all things according to the counsel of His own will, then there must be another power equal to (or above) God. This is idolatry. Any concept of salvation that denies the fact that it is sovereignly administered by God is a perversion of the true gospel.

The nature of this doctrine is such that if any man would remove God's sovereignty he would then be claiming that very right for himself. The same is true if it is said that God is sovereign only in some areas and not in others. Sovereignty, by its very nature, demands complete and total sovereignty or it has no meaning.

These are critical matters beyond the realm of compromise, doubt, or opinions. Remember when Job questioned the "right" of God to cause his suffering, the Lord said, *"Who is this who darkens counsel by words without knowledge?"* (Job 38:2). The very foundation and understanding of our salvation rests on this teaching.

Notice how strong a warning the Bible gives in regard to a denial of this teaching. *"But there were also false prophets among the people, even as there will be false teachers among you, who will secretly bring in destructive heresies, even denying the Lord who bought them, and bring on themselves swift destruction. And many will follow their destructive ways, because of whom the way of truth will be blasphemed."* (II Pet. 2:1-2)

We also see this urgent warning in Jude 4, *"For certain men whose condemnation was written about long ago have secretly slipped in among you. They are godless men, who change the grace of our God into a license for immorality and deny Jesus Christ our only Sovereign and Lord."* (Jude v. 4, NIV)

Where Do You Stand?

We stand at a theological crossroads here. We must either adopt a theology that is man-centered or God-centered. It will become clear through a study of the **Five Points of Calvinism** that the Bible presents only one path of salvation – one which rests on the sovereign grace of God alone. In these studies we will attempt to unveil and understand the errors of Arminianism, but not so we can win some theological battle. The real prize in understanding the sovereign grace of God is the comfort and joy that such salvation brings to our hearts. Only when our salvation is properly understood and believed can there be real assurance of it.

QUESTIONS:

1. Define the word "sovereignty" in one sentence.

   • Write out one Scripture verse that you feel best describes God's sovereignty.

2. If God's sovereignty *over creation* is denied, what are we left with?

3. If God's sovereignty *in salvation* is denied, what are we left with?

4. Explain what is meant when we say that the best way to explain the sovereignty of God is to say that "God is God."

● What is meant by the "self-sufficiency" of God?

● What does the fact that God is the "Creator" have to do with His sovereignty?

5. Why do you think it is difficult for the natural man to accept the fact of God's sovereignty?

6. How do we see the sovereignty of God in the choice of Israel to be His covenant people?

7. If God is sovereign over all His creation, how do we explain the fact that there is so much suffering and trouble in the world? And, if God is sovereign, why are some men lost in unbelief?

8. Indicate how Jesus is also sovereign using John 1 and Ephesians 1.

9. What, in John 3, tells us that the Holy Spirit is sovereign?

10. Why is the denial of God's sovereignty such a serious error?

11. What difference does it make for us as Christians if we believe God is sovereign or not?

12. Some have concluded that if God is sovereign in all things, then man cannot be held responsible for his actions. Explain why this conclusion is wrong (see Romans 9:14ff.).

2

Arminius and the Remonstrants

James Arminius

A Dutch theologian, Jacob Hermanszoon (better known by his Latin name Jacobus Arminius) bears the dubious honor of being the founder of a system of doctrine known as *"Arminianism"* that denies the basic tenets of the gospel and the Reformed faith concerning the matter of the salvation of man and the sovereignty of God. He lived from 1560-1609.

His theological training was in the Reformed faith where he was educated at Leyden, Basle, and Geneva. He studied under Theodore Beza, Calvin's successor in Geneva. In 1588 he returned to Holland to serve as a pastor of a Reformed congregation for fifteen years. Holland had become a center for Calvinism in the sixteenth century.

Arminius vs. Gomarus

Disputes arose in his pastorate as Arminius questioned some of the basic teachings of Calvinism. Here his theology began to adopt the humanist doctrines of Erasmus. Arminius left the pastorate to become a professor at the University of Leyden in 1603. A series of lectures on the subject of "Predestination" led to a heated controversy with the Reformed theologian Francis Gomar (Latin: "Gomarus") who was a skilled and zealous defender of Calvinist orthodoxy and also a professor at the University of Leyden. As this debate spread through the university and churches in Holland, the result was a division into factions known as "Arminian" and "Gomarist" (also called "Strict or

Hyper-Calvinists" who held to the supralapsarian position). Gomar was a member of the Synod of Dort, but did not take a very active part – asking for the floor only once and then to deny that Calvinists taught the doctrine of "absolute predestination." He spent the years from 1618 to 1641 teaching at the University of Groningen.

Following the death of Arminius in 1609, his followers published a "Remonstrance" which spelled out Arminius's position – one contrary to the Reformed faith. Attempts were made through the Dutch government (then in the hands of a liberal politician, Jan van Oldenbarneveldt) to have this issue settled, but this was refused.

Sometime later, however, the Calvinists received the support of Maurice of Nassau, son of William the Silent, who sought a more centralized, monarchical government. Fierce controversy between Maurice and Oldenbarneveldt followed. In 1619 Maurice won the debate, having his opponent judged guilty of treason and subsequently beheaded in that year. This opened the way for a Synod to be held at Dordrecht (shortened to Dort) in which this religious controversy between Arminians and Calvinists could be carefully scrutinized and answered from the Bible.

The Remonstrant Position

The position known as *"Arminianism"* was outlined in a *"Remonstrance"* (a statement of protest) which was published by its proponents in 1610 (see Appendix for the text of their protest). This became known as the *"Five Points of Arminianism."*

This Remonstrance can be summed up by observing its five primary teachings.

(1) God's decree of salvation applies to all who believe in Christ and who persevere in obedience and faith. In other words, God's decree to elect a people unto salvation was general and not particular. All men are chosen, but this can only be effective if man chooses to accept it. Such a doctrine rested on the belief that man, after the Fall, still possessed a *free will.* Their contention was that the fall of our first parents did not result in a total sinful depravity, but enough good was still left in man for him to choose good over evil – to choose Christ as Savior. They took exception to both Martin Luther

(see *Bondage of the Will*, a book by Luther) and John Calvin who were agreed that the Fall of Adam placed all men, with all of their faculties (including the will of man) in bondage to sin and Satan.

The Remonstrants claimed that all men are free to reject or accept, to deny or decide in favor of, salvation by themselves. They did have a doctrine of election, but it was a *"Conditional Election,"* the condition being man's response in faith to God's "offer." God's election unto salvation was determined by *foreseen faith*. God, they claimed, was able to foresee before creation which men would accept His offer of salvation. God chose or elected them on that basis. Certainly God does foresee all things, but this Arminian doctrine leaves God's decrees subject to the condition that sinful men will accept His offer. God's elective decree results from His foresight of what man determines to do with the offer.

(2) Christ died for all men, although only those who "accept" this "offer" in faith are saved. This doctrine of a universal atonement is derived from their first point and rests on the belief that God loves all men to the extent that He wants to save all men. If all men are free by themselves to choose salvation, then not just the message of the gospel, but the actual atoning work of Christ must also be provided for all men, either to accept or reject.

(3) The divine grace of the Holy Spirit is necessary to help men perform any good deed, such as having saving faith in Jesus Christ. Superficially, this sounds right. However, man is free and of sufficient power to accept or reject this work of the Holy Spirit in him. Their doctrine rests on the assumption that God is not sovereign, but for man to be saved there must first be a cooperation between man and God.

(4) God's saving grace is resistible. Since it was God's desire to save all men, He sent His Holy Spirit to try to convince all men to believe. Nevertheless, man can, by his free will, resist this power of God. According to Arminianism, God's plan to save can be frustrated and halted by man's stubborn refusal.

(5) It is possible for true Christians to fall from God's saving grace. This is based upon the assumption that if man is able to come

to salvation by his own will, then it also depends on man to continue to will to be saved. Perseverance in faith is left up to man who may lose this saving faith.

These are the points the Remonstrants introduced into the church as a rejection of the teachings of Calvin and most other prominent reformers of his day. They also contradicted the teachings of the *Heidelberg Catechism* which was written in 1563 and had come into wide use in Reformed churches. Most importantly, these teachings contradicted the clear teachings of the Bible. The Remonstrants insisted that both the *Belgic Confession of Faith* and the *Heidelberg Catechism* must be changed to conform to their views.

QUESTIONS:

1. Where does the term "Arminianism" come from?

   ● Give a brief biography of James Arminius.

2. What is a "Remonstrance?"

3. Below list the doctrines of Calvinism (see Chapter 1) and the corresponding doctrines of the Remonstrants.

   CALVINISM   REMONSTRANTS

1.

2.

3.

4.

5.

4. Why is it impossible for man to be "free" unless he is a Christian?

   ● What is the Christian free to do?

5. Explain below how the teachings of the Remonstrants denied the doctrine of God's "sovereignty."

   ● Modern-day Remonstrants say that they "chose Christ as

their Savior and now must make Jesus their Lord." What is wrong with such a statement *and* why do they arrive at such a conclusion?

6. Answer the following questions *using the Remonstrants' positions*:

- What is the "condition" of election by God?

- Who did Jesus die for?

- Are all saved for whom Jesus died?   Explain:

- If the Holy Spirit can be resisted by man, who is more powerful, the Holy Spirit or man?   Explain your answer:

- Why, according to Arminianism, can people who were once "saved" be lost?

7. If a person who was once "saved" is lost in the end, can we actually call this "salvation?"   Explain your answer:

3

Arminianism and the
Canons of Dort

The Freedom of Arminianism

The Arminians claim that faith is a free and responsible act of man; it cannot be caused by God. Faith essentially comes about independently of God. Subsequently, man can choose if he will be saved or not, and God's decrees have been determined by what He foresaw to be man's actions. They conclude that the ability to believe must be universal. Every man has the innate freedom and ability to come to saving faith if he so desires in order to prove that God is a just God.

Man's faith, according to the Arminian logic, is his gift to God, rather than God's gift to man. The real cause of salvation is the sinner's choice of Christ, not God's choice of the sinner. His salvation depends on *his acceptance* of (his decision to accept) the work of Christ, not on his being *made acceptable* through the work of Christ. Ephesians 1:6 clearly gives all praise to God for His grace, *"by which he hath made us accepted in the Beloved* (Christ)."

Christ's sacrifice, the Arminian alleges, made it *possible* for all men to be saved, but is *effective* only if man chooses to accept it. If no man accepts it, then the death of Christ was all in vain. His sacrifice did not actually remove any man's sins, but *only provided for the possibility* of salvation. God would pardon sin only on the condition that man chooses to believe.

Not only is the "free will" of man wrongly elevated by the Arminian, but as a consequence, the sovereignty of God is repudiated. As long as man holds the "veto power" in himself, he is declaring himself more powerful than God. If God wants to save man and is prohibited by man's refusal, then man becomes equal to God. If the Holy Spirit's work of grace can be refused, then man has God at his mercy.

Unintended Consequences of Arminianism

The lamentable result of Arminianism is that it eliminates all *assurance* of salvation to those who now believe. Where is the comfort in a salvation that a man may lose by his own weakness? Yet, this is the logical result of this theology. If man can choose salvation by his own free will, he can also lose it by his own free will. While the Arminian does believe that God will always accept the sacrifice of Christ as the atonement for sin, he has no hope that the instrument of faith will remain with man.

If the teachings of Arminianism were true, *no one would be saved*, and the whole plan of God in sending His Son to save would be a total failure. This is because the Scriptures deny the ability of man to ever come to God apart from God's own sovereign, enabling grace. And, secondly, even if man were able to accept Christ as his Savior by his own power, he could never persevere in this faith on his own and would be lost in the end.

Arminianism distorts the person of God. He is presented as a very weak and unjust God. If He wants to save all men and cannot, He is no longer Almighty. If He sent Jesus to die for the sins of all men, and then some are still lost because of their refusal to believe, then He is not able to carry out His own will. And if Jesus atoned for the sins of all men, and some are lost, then God is unjust in sending some to hell, for in doing so He is punishing them for sins that were already paid for ("double jeopardy").

A Humanist Theology

Arminianism is the product of *humanism* which exemplifies the sinful pride of depraved man since the Fall. In humanism, everything begins and ends with man. Man is at the center of his own existence, not God. Fallen human nature longs to be autonomous – a law unto itself in all things. The Renaissance between the fourteenth and seventeenth centuries produced many good results, of which the Reformation is a part. But, negatively, it placed the abilities and inherent freedom of man as a central part of its thinking. This played into the hands of fallen man's thinking – to be as wise as God. It became extremely popular to apply humanism's teachings to theology. Men have clamored for the freedom to make their own sovereign choices ever since the Garden of Eden.

Sin has so blinded man that he does not realize that *the only freedom he has as an unregenerate man is the freedom to sin*, since he is in bondage to sin. Yet, Scripture tells us that real freedom can come only to the disciple of Jesus Christ who knows the Truth. John 8:31,32,36 teaches, *"Then Jesus said to those Jews who believed Him, If you abide in My word, you are My disciples indeed. And you shall know the truth, and the truth shall make you* free. *Therefore if the Son makes you free, you shall be free indeed."*

Real Christian freedom is the freedom to submit to the Word of God. The freedom that man longs for comes only through the redemption of Jesus Christ, when man becomes free from sin and bondage to Satan. Even after redemption, man becomes a servant. *"And having been set free from sin, you became slaves of righteousness. But now having been set free from sin, and having become slaves of God, you have your fruit to holiness, and the end, everlasting life."* (Rom. 6:18,22) Man's will is never free to do as it pleases. It is either in bondage to sin or to Christ.

No fallen human being wants to admit that he is a slave or is in bondage – especially, to say that their will is in bondage to Satan. The Jews of Jesus' day claimed that they were free and never in bondage to anyone, just because they were the children of Abraham. *"They answered Him, We are Abraham's descendants, and have never been in bondage to anyone. How can you say, You will be made free?"* (Jn. 8:33). Jesus was talking about a greater emancipation – namely, a freedom from the curse and power of sin and bondage to Satan so that man can serve God as He was created to do, *"For we are His workmanship, created in Christ Jesus for good works, which God*

prepared beforehand that we should walk in them." (Eph. 2:10).
Arminianism denies the bondage of the will which causes us to ask,
how can man truly rejoice in the redemption and freedom that Christ
speaks about?

Questions Raised

While we cannot say that all those who hold to the teachings
of Arminianism are lost, we must at least conclude that if they are
saved it is in spite of their theology. What they attribute to themselves
is in fact a work of God's grace in them. Many Arminians still trust
that it is the blood of Jesus Christ alone that cleanses them from sin.
They do say that salvation comes by grace through faith (howbeit they
define these terms quite differently). It is not our purpose or prerogative to judge another's ultimate salvation. We will leave it to God to
judge whether a person who denies His sovereign grace will inherit
the kingdom of heaven.

Our purpose in this study is not to judge the salvation of
others, but to exalt and glorify God as He should be in the salvation of
His people. Yet, we certainly can judge whether a theology is right or
wrong by the teachings of Scripture. We must have a concern for the
Truth. And we must unashamedly tell the Truth as the Scriptures
reveal it.

It is our hope that anyone who has accepted the Arminian
theology will search the Scriptures again to re-examine the basis for
true faith. Is it not the proper attitude for sinners to totally humble
themselves and confess that they are unable to love God until He has
first loved them? What could be so painful about relying totally on the
grace of God for salvation? Is it so difficult to say, "Nothing in my
hands I bring"? Or, is it really so dreadful to confess that our God is
sovereign? Is it not biblical to give God all the glory for our salvation?

Arminians often label Calvinists as being *"determinists"* (God
has determined all things, so man is nothing more than a mere puppet).
This is a false label. It is the intention of Calvinists to simply declare
the things that God has determined which can neither be denied,
deleted, or destroyed (Dan. 11:36; Acts 2:23; 4:28; 17:26; etc.) Every
Christian, not just the Calvinist, is called to give witness to those

truths.

To our Arminian friends, we hope that a study of the teachings of Calvinism will help to alleviate these misapprehensions. It is our ardent desire that you will join us in this most precious faith. We confess that we need to search the Scriptures daily and continue to grow in knowledge and trust. If Calvinism is the teaching of Scripture, as we believe it is, then every Christian must accept it. When we say that the Reformed faith is the truest expression of biblical Christianity, this is not out of boastfulness, but out of a deep sense of reverence and humility. Because the doctrines of our faith are derived from the Word of God, we neither doubt them nor apologize for them. It is our greatest joy to receive them and teach them.

The Synod of Dort

The charges and proposed doctrinal changes forwarded by the Remonstrants had to be answered for the sake of attributing all glory to God and for the purity and unity of the church. On November 13, 1618, an international meeting of church leaders was convened by order of the States-General of Holland. It met at Dordrecht and came to be called the Synod of Dort.

From Holland, Germany, the Palatinate, England, and Switzerland 84 delegates and 18 secular commissioners met for seven months to study the Bible on these matters. After 154 sessions they had produced statements answering point by point the Remonstrant's Arminian doctrines. The Synod concluded its work on May 9, 1619.

Results of the Synod of Dort

The document which emerged from this meeting was called "The Canons of Dort." It was a list of theological statements (canons) carefully affirming and clarifying the doctrines of Scripture which were presently held by the Reformed Churches. In addition, they answered various objections which men had or would raise. My own summary of the *Canons of Dort* appears in the Appendix of this book.

The Synod of Dort condemned the teachings of the Arminians as being out of accord with Scripture. *The Belgic Confession of Faith* and the *Heidelberg Catechism* were reaffirmed as being orthodox, biblical confessions for the Church. They also produced the Church Order of Dort, which we will not get into for our purposes here.

The reaction against Arminianism at that time was rather severe. Some, such as Hugo Grotius, were imprisoned or banished so long as they continued following the Remonstrant position. After a few years there was a negative reaction to this severe treatment and a certain toleration was given to the Arminian Remonstrants to hold and espouse their teachings.

Today, with the widespread influence of Arminianism, we are shocked by the fact that Arminianism was once such a minority position. Attitudes have reversed tremendously. Arminianism is widely accepted by the church of today, and the Calvinists are often ostracized.

Arminianism spread, as Calvinism had, to many countries of the world. In England an Anti-Calvinist movement was spurred on by Arminians. John Wesley bought into the Arminian doctrines and greatly influenced the Methodist church. Churches generally did not adopt the title "Arminian" as the name for their churches. Arminian doctrines are the confession of churches identified by various different names. To a lessor extent we may say the same of Calvinism.

Today, we find that the vast majority of Protestant churches, whether liberal or evangelical, have adopted all or part of the teachings of the Remonstrants. That which may grieve us most is that even among many individuals and congregations who claim a Reformed heritage, Arminianism has gained a foothold and an appeal such that the doctrines of Calvinism are often ignored or rejected completely. It is pathetic that in many circles the children of the Reformed heritage are no longer having these truths taught or explained to them. If these are doctrines taught in Scripture, let us never be ashamed to hold firmly to them and teach them to others.

Some aberrations within the system of Calvinism (such as "Hyper-Calvinism", which will be examined in the course of this study) have led to a false characterization of all Calvinists. For the most part, the rejection of the validity of Calvinism has come from those whose faith and life cannot tolerate the notion of a sovereign God. The result is that the word "Calvinist" (or sometimes "Puritan") has become a label used by many people to characterize it as a false, fanatical, and stilted set of beliefs that hardly anyone, except for a few misled "cultists," take seriously today.

It is up to us to study the Scriptures and then set the record straight and continue to spread the gospel that truly proclaims salvation by grace through faith in Jesus Christ. To the student of the Scriptures, this is our challenge.

QUESTIONS:

1. How are the teachings of "humanism" and "Arminianism" similar as to their basis?

2. If you were to find one major error in Arminianism, what would that be?

3. Explain how the system of Arminianism actually denies the atoning work of Christ?

● What are some of the terrible results of Arminian doctrines?

4. What is meant when we say that "if Arminianism is right then nobody is saved"?

● What does the Arminian mean when he says that his faith is his gift to God?

● Untangle this puzzle of Arminianism according to their own teaching: "Christ died for everyone, but he did not die to save any- one."

5. What was the purpose of the Synod of Dort?

● When did it meet?

● Who was present at the Synod?

5. What document was produced to refute the teachings of the Remonstrant Arminians?

● These doctrines are also sometimes called "_____

_____

___."

6. Identify:

    ● Jacob Hermanszoon:

    ● Maurice of Nassau:

    ● Francis Gomar:

    ● Hugo Grotius:

7. How do you explain the popularity of Arminianism today?

    ● How can both liberals and some "conservative evangelicals" come to agreement in this area?

8. How do you think the Arminian doctrines affect the way mission work is done in Arminian churches?

9. How would you answer the charge that Calvinism is "deterministic?"

10. Why is there no real assurance of salvation in Arminian doctrine?

11. According to the Bible, where does true freedom come from?

    ● Is it possible for a slave to have freedom before someone sets him free?　Explain:

    ● Explain the type of freedom that the Christian has.

4

The Doctrine of Total Depravity
Part 1

The Flower of Calvinism

Among many who have a Reformed heritage, the flower of Calvinism – the **TULIP** – is wilting. In examining each of the doctrines of Calvinism more closely we will follow the usual order of the acrostic

"T U L I P"

Total Depravity

Unconditional Election

Limited Atonement

Irresistible Grace

Perseverance of the Saints

The Canons of Dort were written in a different order from

what we will study since its authors answered the Arminian Remonstrance in the same order in which it was presented to them.

The doctrine of *total depravity* is the first of the *Five Points of Calvinism* that we will study. We might also call this the doctrine of *total inability*. Since this doctrine is very foundational to all the rest, we should first summarize the Arminian position so we can more clearly contrast it with the doctrines of Scripture as set forth in the Canons of Dort.

Free Will of Arminianism

The Arminian doctrine states that, although human nature was seriously affected by the Fall, man has not been left in a state of total sinfulness and inability. God graciously enables every sinner to repent and believe, but he does so in such a manner as not to interfere with man's supposed freedom. Thus, they are able to speak about the need for "grace," but it is not total or sovereign grace. God cannot give it unless man has decided to accept it by his own free will. Salvation is by grace as far as its *provision* is concerned, but not as far as its *application* is concerned. It is this latter teaching which we reject as unbiblical.

They contend that man has a free will, and his eternal destiny depends on how he uses it. Arminianism contends that man's freedom consists in his ability to choose good over evil in spiritual matters; his will is not enslaved along with his sinful nature. The will of man was not totally corrupted by the Fall. The sinner has the power either to *cooperate* with God's Holy Spirit and be regenerated or *resist* God's gracious attempts and perish. The lost sinner needs the Spirit's assistance, but he does not have to be regenerated by the Holy Spirit *before* he can believe. Arminians say that faith is man's act and it precedes the new birth. After faith comes, man receives the gift of the Holy Spirit. Hence you may hear the description that a person is a "born again Christian" (when in fact, there are no Christians who are not born again). Faith, in their estimation, is a gift we give to God; it is man's contribution to his salvation.

We are able to observe the consequences of this doctrine when we see the Arminian as he engages in mission work. Much of the emphasis in that work is directed at the *proper methodologies* that will cause man to change his mind and believe. This may often be done to the exclusion of or at the expense of biblical doctrines. Many of the methods that we observe center around a variety of entertainment, logical and emotional appeals, and sensationalism that are designed to convince the sinner to repent and believe. It would be their claim that if we could just get a person in a room and have enough time, he would eventually break down and become a believer.

In Arminianism there is no actual admission that the will of man is enslaved by nature to serve the Devil. Yet the Scriptures say that man's will is unable by itself to choose Christ. *"Because the carnal mind is enmity against God; for it is not subject to the law of God, nor indeed **can** be. So then, those who are in the flesh **cannot** please God. "* (Rom. 8:7,8 emphasis mine) The word *"flesh"* here does not refer to the physical body, but the sinful nature which we inherit from Adam, as opposed to the *"spiritual"* nature which we are given by the Holy Spirit of God (cf. Rom. 8:1).

It is the Arminian position that sin has "hurt" man's original state badly, but the will of man has escaped this total sinful corruption. So, within man there is a strange mixture of good and evil, each with an equal opportunity to win out. Hence, we hear the expression even in reference to the unregenerate person, "There's a little bit of good in everyone." They interpret Romans 7:16ff., not as the life of a believer (as Paul was when he wrote this), but as the life of someone struggling to become a believer. Man, then, is not dead in sin (Eph. 2:1ff.), but he is just very sick – sick unto death, but not dead in sin. They claim that man still has the ears to hear and the eyes to see, despite what the Scriptures say.

We should add here that man does indeed have a will after the Fall. He is still a free moral agent; able to make choices in his life. The problem is not an absence of a will, but the total depravity of the will which makes it prone to all evil in all things. Man's will always chooses to serve himself and not God until he receives the Holy Spirit. "He is prone to hate God and his neighbor." (*Heidelberg Catechism* Q. 5) What may appear to be a good work in man's eyes, is not a good work in God's eyes unless it proceeds out of true faith, is performed according to the Law of God, and is done for the glory of God (*Heidelberg Catechism* Q. 91).

Sin: Intensive and Extensive

A study of "total depravity" should include the realization that the natural (unregenerate) man is not as bad as he could be in his actions. If that were the case then the unbeliever would be constantly in an open physical rebellion and confrontation with the church all of his days. We can see that this is not the case. Many unbelievers can be "good neighbors" to Christians. Many discoveries by the heathen in science, medicine, and learning have been beneficial to Christians. Sin is *not totally intensive*, but is held in check by God.

This is a part of what is sometimes called God's "common grace" (not to be confused with "saving grace") whereby God restrains the heathen from being as bad as they could be, and actually are, in their fallen nature. For example, an unbelieving heart surgeon may be given abilities from God to benefit many. Likewise heathen nations are held in check from performing all the evil they are capable of. God may even use them as He did in the Old Testament to instruct or discipline His people. Notice just a few examples: Deut. 32:21; Judges 3:1-4; I Kg. 11:14*ff*.; Jer. 5:15; 6:22,23; Luke 19:41*ff*.

By restraining unbelievers from doing what is really in their hearts, carnal men are even able to obey some of the letter of the law (howbeit for the wrong reasons since they do not seek to give glory to God in this). See Romans 2:14-16. God restrains this evil in order that the gospel may have free course, and His elect people may have a measure of physical peace in this life. See Matthew 24:22-24.

We should never conclude that if the unbeliever is able to perform some things which appear to be good in the eyes of men, that these same actions are good or glorifying in the eyes of God. The good things that God gives to all men – sunshine, rain, and various pleasures – require a proper response. They should be used to serve God out of thankfulness. This the unbeliever cannot and will not do. In the end, the unthankfulness and unfaithfulness of the unbeliever in the things God has given to him will be called into account. He will be shown to be a sinful steward – using his time, talents, and God's gifts only for his own selfish purposes, the end of which is condemnation (see the Parable of the Talents in Matt. 25, especially vv. 24-30; cf. 25:41-46).

We might add here that the believer is not as good as he should be either, even though he is reborn by the Spirit of God and in Christ he is declared to be totally righteous. In reality his life falls far short of the new nature that is his in Christ. See how Paul describes this struggle in Romans 7 when he admits *"For what I am doing, I do not understand. For what I will to do, that I do not practice; but what I hate, that I do,"* and again, *"For the good that I will to do, I do not do; but the evil I will not to do, that I practice."* (Rom. 7:15,19) What this says is that our old sinful nature still cleaves to us as long as we are in this body. Yet, the believer does not have this sin imputed to him, *"Blessed is he whose transgression is forgiven, Whose sin is covered. Blessed is the man to whom the LORD does not impute iniquity, And in whose spirit there is no guile."* (Ps. 32:1,2), but rather the righteousness of Christ is imputed to him (see Rom. 4:8; 5:18-21; II Cor. 5:19, 21).

The other aspect of total depravity is the *extent* to which man is depraved. This is *total*. We speak here of two areas. First, it extends to *all the offspring of Adam*, and, secondly, sin has corrupted the *entire nature of man*, in all of its aspects. In this regard it is worth looking at the clear teaching of Romans 3:10-18, 23:

> *"As it is written: There is **none** righteous, no, **not one**; there is **none** who understands; there is **none** who seeks after God. They have **all** gone out of the way; they have together become unprofitable; there is **none** who does good, no, **not one**. Their throat is an open tomb; with their tongues they have practiced deceit; The poison of asps is under their lips; Whose mouth is full of cursing and bitterness. Their feet are swift to shed blood; destruction and misery are in their ways; and the way of peace they have not known. There is **no fear of God** before their eyes."* *"for **all have sinned** and fall short of the glory of God."* (Emphasis mine)

Man's *entire nature* is completely corrupt, perverse, and sinful throughout. He is naturally prone, inclined, and bent on sinning against both God and his neighbor. Man's nature is *depraved* (literally, "crooked"). Every part of man is adversely affected by this sinful nature which he inherited from Adam (Rom. 5:12) – his heart, mind, soul, and strength. His will or desire is not free to act either in a good or a bad way. It is totally enslaved to do evil in and of itself. In other words, there is not some small spark of good that remains after the Fall – no small light that was not extinguished by sin. *Heidelberg Catechism* Q. 8 asks, *"But are we so depraved that we are completely incapable of any good and prone to all evil?"* To which it answers, *"Yes, unless we are born again by the Spirit of God."* (See also *Heidelberg Catechism* Q.'s 5-7). Fallen man's ears cannot hear and understand; his eyes cannot see and perceive. He is *dead* in his trespasses and sins as Ephesians 2:1 says. Man is not sick unto death as the Arminian would have us believe, but really, spiritually dead.

We should say a word, however, about an often misunderstood teaching in the *Canons of Dort* (3rd and 4th Heads of Doctrine, Article 4) which states, *"There remain, however, in man since the fall, the glimmerings of natural understanding, whereby he retains some knowledge of God, of natural things, and of the difference between good and evil, and shows some regard for virtue and for good outward behavior."*

Some have wrongly interpreted this to mean that man is not totally depraved, but there remains in him a glimmer of goodness. That would be to miss the intended meaning of this article. What the writers are speaking about is Romans 1:19-21 which tell us that God reveals his eternal power and divinity to all men: *"because what may be known of God is manifest in them, for God has shown it to them. For since the creation of the world His invisible attributes are clearly seen, being understood by the things that are made, even His eternal power and Godhead, so that they are without excuse, because, although they knew God, they did not glorify Him as God, nor were thankful, but became futile in their thoughts, and their foolish hearts were darkened."*

All men are able to observe the hand of God in the world in which they live, yet, the unregenerate person will deny that it is of God. This knowledge of God is present because man was created in the image of God. John Calvin calls this retention of the knowledge of God, *"sense of divinity"* (Latin: *"divinitatis sensum"*; see Calvin's *Institutes of the Christian Religion*, Book 1, Ch. 3-5). This is based on the teaching of Rom. 1:21 where, in addressing the condition of all men, Paul says, *"Because, although they knew God..."*)

The *Canons of Dort* point out that this *"glimmering of understanding ... so far from being sufficient to bring him to a saving knowledge of God and to true conversion"* actually demonstrates the totality of man's depraved nature and renders him without excuse before God. While unregenerate man still has this knowledge of God, he denies God and refuses to glorify or thank Him (Rom. 1:21). Instead of teaching that man has some good in himself, it teaches just the opposite – it underscores the totality of man's depravity. Man's corruption in sin is so severe that *even when he knows God, he still rebels against Him.* Read all of Romans 1:18-32 and also Articles 4-6 of the *Canons of Dort.*

It is this *"sense of divinity"* which gives the believer and the unbeliever a "point of contact" (which Dr. Cornelius Van Til called the *"Anknöpfungspunkt"*) or a sort of "common ground." Both know that there is a God. However, all similarity ends there, because the believer confesses, glorifies, and serves God while the unregenerate denies and rejects God.

The Origin of Sin

The origin of this sinful nature comes from the sin of Adam in paradise. Adam acted as the *representative head* of the whole human race when he disobeyed God and came under the condemnation of God. God had clearly told Adam that he could eat of all of the trees of the Garden of Eden except for one – the *"tree of the knowledge of good and evil... for in the day that you eat of it you shall surely die."* (Gen. 2:17) Genesis 3 relates the sad truth of how Adam followed the example of Eve, who listened to Satan, and ate of the forbidden fruit. God had also clearly warned Adam that death would come immediately upon disobedience. Adam ate and died (Gen. 3:6; Rom. 5:12, 17-19).

This death was of two types. Immediately he died *spiritually.*

He was separated from fellowship with God and came under the curse of eternal condemnation. In the second place, *physically*, from that moment he began to die (and he did die 930 years later). The fact that man grows old and dies is due to the sinful nature that he has inherited from Adam. This first sin caused not just a sentence of death to hang over Adam, but it corrupted his whole nature, and all of his descendants likewise. The righteousness, holiness, and perfect knowledge of God died in Adam to the extent that each of these attributes was totally corrupted by sin.

Since Adam was a representative for the whole human race, in the sin of Adam all men have sinned and stand guilty before God and cursed by God. Romans 5:12 tells us clearly, *"Therefore, just as through one man sin entered the world, and death through sin, and thus death spread to all men, because all sinned."* Paul also says, in reference to the curse of God's eternal condemnation, that all men were by nature *"dead in trespasses and sins,"* and *"the children of wrath."* (Eph. 2:1, 3)

While it might be objected that it is not fair that we should inherit the sin of someone else, let us be careful to note that in the same way that all men inherit Adam's sin, the believer also inherits the righteousness of someone else – Jesus Christ. Both Adam's sin and Christ's righteousness are "imputed." Romans 5:15 and 17 tell us, *"But the free gift is not like the offense. For if by the one man's offense many died, much more the grace of God and the gift by the grace of the one Man, Jesus Christ, abounded to many."* and, *"For if by the one man's offense death reigned through the one, much more those who receive abundance of grace and of the gift of righteousness will reign in life through the One, Jesus Christ."*

This doctrine of *inborn sin* (or, original sin) is denied by the Pelagians who believe that man is born in a neutral state – neither good nor evil. This heresy was the product of Pelagius, a British monk, who was a popular preacher in Rome in the 400's A.D. He taught that every man may live free from sin if he wills. Man's will was absolutely unaffected by the Fall. His present condition is like that of Adam before the Fall. Man becomes a sinner as he matures and begins to imitate the sins of those around him. Pure Pelagianism would say that an infant who died in infancy would have to be saved automatically because he would not yet have committed a sin.

In the *Mennonite Confession of Faith*, (adopted by the Mennonite General Conference August 22, 1963, Herald Press, Scottdale, PA) Art. 4, this Pelagian doctrine is stated as follows: *"Although men are sinners by nature because of Adam's fall, they are not guilty of his sin. Those who perish eternally do so only because of their own sin."* And again, *"We believe that children are born with a nature which will manifest itself as sinful as they mature."* While there is an admission of the *predisposition to sin*, man is not born with either the guilt or the curse of Adam's sin on him.

While all Arminianism does not say exactly that, they maintain that man did not fall in the totality of his being. His will is still free from sin. Most Arminianism is a form of Pelagianism which we call Semi-Pelagianism. Semi-Pelagianism admits that there is inability (a limited form which does not affect the will) attached to our inherited sin, but man is not responsible for this inability and therefore cannot be held guilty for it. There are some Arminians who teach that infants are innocent and therefore are saved if they die in infancy. Some even maintain that there is a "baby heaven" where all infants enter upon death. The Bible teaches no such thing.

Eternal condemnation is God's just reward for all men in fallen Adam. On the other hand, by grace alone, *"There is therefore now no condemnation to those who are in Christ Jesus, who do not walk according to the flesh, but according to the Spirit."* (Rom. 8:1).

Three Steps of Imputation

Imputation means that something has been added to another's account. The act of imputation is directed to and for man by another. In other words, man is not active – not the author – in the matter of imputation, but passive. There are three steps in imputation that we should remember.

First, Adam's sin is imputed to us by God. As we have seen, this is because Adam was the representative head of all mankind. When he fell, all his posterity had the guilt of his sin added to their account, so that they are all liable to the punishment of everlasting death. This imputed sin is not just the corruption of man's nature, but actual guilt that carries a death sentence with it. John 3:18 speaks of the unbeliever as being *"condemned already."*

Romans 5 teaches that *death reigns in us* because of the sin of Adam imputed to us: *"by the one man's offense many died"* (v. 15); *"The judgment which came from one offense resulted in condemnation"* (v. 16); *"By one man's offence death reigned through the one"* (v. 17); *"Therefore as through one man's offence judgment came to all men, resulting in   condemnation"* (v. 18); and *"For as by one man's disobedience many were made sinners"* (v. 19).

Secondly, the sin of God's people is imputed to, or laid upon Christ. Man did not do this, but the LORD *"has laid on Him the iniquity of us all"* (see Isaiah 53:4-12 for a picture of Christ vicariously bearing the sins of His people). In the Old Testament sacrifice, the person bringing a sacrifice had to lay his hand on the sacrifice and pronounce his sins upon it. The animal was then sacrificed as a *type* of the true substitute for sin, which is Christ alone. The important thing to see is that sin was symbolically transferred to the sacrificial animal (Lev 17:11). In the same way God imputes our sins to His own Son, the perfect sacrificial Lamb.

It was *not our sinfulness* that was imputed to Christ. Otherwise He would have been a sinner. But, it was our sin, guilt, and punishment for sin – the curse of hell – that was imputed to Him. Jesus became the bearer of our sin. Isaiah 53:6 says, *"and the LORD hath laid on him the iniquity of us all."* John 1:29 describes Christ as *"the Lamb of God who takes away the sin of the world."* Paul says in II Cor. 5:21, *"For He* [God the Father] *made Him* [Christ] *who knew no sin to be sin for us, that we might become the righteousness of God in Him."* Galatians 3:13 says, *"Christ has redeemed us from the curse of the law, having become a curse for us...."* *"Christ was offered once to bear the sins of many,"* says Hebrews 9:28. And I Peter 2:24 says about Christ: *"Who himself bore our sins in his own body on the tree...."*

And thirdly, the righteousness of Christ is imputed to His people. On the cross Christ satisfied the justice of God against the sin which he bore. As the sinless Lamb of God, He laid down His life.

The only ground of our justification is in the fact that the satisfaction, righteousness, and holiness of Christ becomes our righteousness before God. *Heidelberg Catechism* Q. 60 teaches how we are righteous before God: *"Only by true faith in Jesus Christ: that is, although my conscience accuses me, that I have grievously sinned against all the commandments of God and have never kept any of them, and am still prone always to all evil; yet God, without any merit of mine, of mere grace, grants and imputes to me the perfect satisfaction, righteousness, and holiness of Christ, as if I had never committed nor had any sins, and had myself accomplished all the obedience which Christ has fulfilled for me; if only I accept such benefit with a believing heart."* See also questions 61 and 62.

Arminian doctrine teaches that we are justified by God on the ground of our faith in Christ. The Bible, however, teaches that we are justified only *on the ground of the perfect righteousness of Jesus Christ.* This righteousness is ours only by grace through faith.

Romans 3:24,25 states, *"being justified freely by His grace through the redemption that is in Christ Jesus, whom God set forth to be a propitiation by His blood, through faith, to demonstrate His righteousness...."* (see also Rom. 5:1, 9,19; 8:1; 10:4.) I Corinthians 1:30 states, *"But of Him you are in Christ Jesus, who became for us wisdom from God – and righteousness and sanctification and redemption."* Christ was made sin for us, *"that we might become the righteousness of God in him"* (II Cor. 5:21). And Philippians 3:9 teaches, *"and be found in Him, not having my own righteousness, which is from the law, but that which is through faith in Christ, the righteousness which is from God by faith."*

We might just add here that once God has imputed the righteousness of Christ to us, He no longer imputes our actual sins to us (see Psalm 32:1,2). The reason for this is that they are already covered or atoned for by the blood of Christ. II Cor. 5:19 says, *"that is, that God was in Christ reconciling the world to Himself, not imputing their trespasses to them...."* *"Blessed is the man to whom the Lord does not impute iniquity..."* (Ps. 32:2).

In each case of imputation, it is an action performed by God, not man. God acts upon man – then man acts in repentance and faith, by the grace and power of God.

QUESTIONS

1. Explain the difference between depravity as "intensive" and "extensive."

2. How is the image of God in man affected by the Fall?

3. In what way is the Arminian teaching of depravity NOT total?

4. How "free" is man after the Fall?

       • Is a dead man free to come back to life anytime he wants to? Explain your answer:

5. In what way does the Arminian position of "free will" deny the following:

       • Grace:

       • Sovereignty of God:

       • Assurance of salvation:

6. How did all men become sinners because of Adam's sin?

       • Write out a Scripture verse that teaches this.

7. How would you explain the matter of "fairness" when it comes to how man inherited his sinful nature from Adam?

8. List the three forms of "Imputation" AND give at least one Scripture verse that teaches each.

    1.

    2.

    3.

9. Is faith an act of man?

       • Does God hold man responsible for his belief or unbelief?

       • What must take place before man can believe?

10. Explain just how bad totally depraved man is.

Explain what is meant by the *"glimmerings of natural light"* in the Canons of Dort.

- Where in the Bible does that teaching come from?

- Why is this not a denial of total depravity?

- What is the "point of contact" that believers have with unbelievers?

11. If we deny total depravity, how does that affect the methods that are used in evangelism?

12. What is "Pelagianism?"

- Why is it wrong?

- What is "Semi-Pelagianism" and how do the Arminians share in that doctrine?

5

The Doctrine of Total Depravity
Part 2

The Necessity of Regeneration Before Faith

Totally depraved man is not able to do anything that is spiritually good unless his nature is first reborn or renewed. This regeneration is the gift of God by His Holy Spirit. It does not proceed from within man himself nor is it initiated in any way by man. He certainly can do nothing to earn or merit his salvation, nor does he deserve God's desire to give him salvation. He does not have the freedom to will to do this. Man has neither the natural *ability* nor the *desire* to choose to be saved and serve God. The Scripture makes it clear that fallen man is *"under bondage"* to sin and therefore is bound to serve Satan (the result of which is death). See Romans 6: 16-23.

A man is free only insofar as his slavery allows him (as far as his chains will reach). Man is allowed to love God after the fall, but he is not able or desirous to do this because of the depraved nature of his heart and mind. So, fallen man does what comes naturally – he "freely" sins and delights in it (Romans 1:21-32). He is a willing slave to sin, and will even deny that he is a slave and needs to be redeemed. Cell mates on "death row" may claim to be free as long as they can walk six feet across their cell, but they are only free (in their own minds) within the limits of their bondage which leads to death.

Anyone in bondage or slavery is not free to do anything he

pleases, unless he is first *set free*. The Israelites who were slaves in Egypt were not free to walk away until God released them. They were not free to walk away from their slavery and serve God as He had commanded them in His covenant. Nor did they have a desire to be free and worship God. They even rejected Moses who had come to lead them to freedom; and they later expressed their desire to go back to slavery.

The Scriptures tell us that the natural or unregenerate man is *"dead in his trespasses and sins"* (Eph. 2:1*ff*.). A *"dead"* person simply cannot decide or choose to come back to life, unless he is raised from the dead and given life by a greater power outside of himself. The same is true spiritually. Fallen sinners are dead and can no more come back to life by themselves than Lazarus could come from the grave apart from the life-giving power in the voice of Jesus. A dead man cannot suddenly decide by himself to take of the water of life in Jesus Christ, no matter how much he needs it. He does not even have a thirsting for it.

Sin is a spiritual blindness which darkens the heart (Eph. 4:18; II Cor. 3:14; 4:4). No matter how brightly the light of the gospel may shine in the eyes of the unbeliever, he cannot see it any more than a blind man can see the light of the sun (see Matt. 6:23). Likewise, you may shout in the ears of a deaf man to no avail. Until he is given *"ears to hear,"* he cannot receive the gospel with understanding or faith.

Man is Not a Co-Operator in Coming to Salvation

If man's depravity and inability were not total and he was able to respond to the call of the gospel before the work of regeneration, then we would have to conclude that his salvation was a cooperative venture – God provided it and man accepted it on his own. God does His part and man does his.

In human affairs this may sound plausible, but the Scriptures clearly tell us that this is impossible for man to do in the matter of his salvation. Paul reminds us in Romans 8:7,8, *"Because the carnal mind is enmity against God: for it is not subject to the law of God, neither indeed can be. So then they that are in the flesh cannot please God"* (*"flesh"* here refers to the sinful nature of man in Adam).

Before man can come to repentance and faith and perform any work of thanksgiving acceptable in the sight of God, he must be born again by the Spirit of God. See John 3:3,5; Romans 12:1-3; and *Heidelberg Catechism* Q. 8. It is the Spirit of God who breathes life into our spiritually dead corpses and then He adopts us to be the sons of God. John points out we were *"born, not of blood, nor of the will of the flesh, nor of the will of man, but of God."* (Jn. 1:13)

Apart from this life-giving power of God, all that a man hears in the gospel is foolishness to him (I Cor. 1:18, 23). That is understandable in the light of what we read in I Cor. 2:14, *"But the natural man does not receive the things of the Spirit of God, for they are foolishness to him; nor can he know them, because they are spiritually discerned."*

The Importance of Understanding Man's Sinful Nature

There may be some who say at this point, "What's the difference what we believe with regard to this doctrine? Even Arminians say that Christ is their Savior, and they do believe in regeneration by the Holy Spirit." These things may be true. But, if we look at the teachings of the Arminian closer, we will discover that if man is not totally depraved and helpless in the deadness of his sin, then he is not really saved by Christ alone at all. It is a cooperation between God and man – partly by grace and partly by works.

If man is good enough to will and choose salvation on his own, the Scriptures are wrong about his dead condition. And if his salvation is a cooperative venture – that is, God provides and man takes if he chooses – then we see a serious departure from the teaching of Ephesians 2:8 and 9 which teach us that *"For by grace you have been saved through faith, and that not of yourselves; it is the gift of God, not of works, lest anyone should boast."* Notice that it is *"faith"* which man cannot attain by himself. We may glory in the cross of Christ as a gift to us (Gal. 6:14), but we may not boast in salvation as though *we* had contributed to it even so much as to say we could accept it by ourselves. At times in the history of redemption God used men to carry out his purposes, but never does God ever require the help of sinful man to provide salvation!

The gift of salvation should be viewed somewhat differently than a common birthday gift. In our normal lives when we are given a gift, we are both able and look forward to receiving it. In our salvation, because there is a natural hatred between God and man, and a blindness which hides the gift, we neither *desire* it nor are we *able* even to receive it of ourselves. A vital part of the gift of our salvation is that God *enables us* to see the gift and believe.

Some Common Errors in this Doctrine

We often hear from the Arminians that God did all He could do when He provided salvation. Now His hands are tied! and He can do nothing but wait for man to accept His gift. It takes a great deal of arrogance to say such a thing, yet, in order to maintain the freedom of man, the Arminian has enslaved the Almighty God.

In Arminianism, it is only after the natural man has made this so-called "decision for Christ," that God can send His Holy Spirit to him as a gift. But, it is simply not true that faith comes before regeneration. As a matter of fact it is impossible. As Jesus told Nicodemus, without being born again he could not even *"see the kingdom of God."* (Jn. 3:3) See what the Scriptures say in Eph. 4:17,18; Rom 3:11,18; 8:6-8. Without the Holy Spirit operating within man, his appetite is only for evil (Gen. 6:5) or as the book of Job says that man, *"drinks iniquity like water."* (Job 15:16)

Classic Arminianism comes to these conclusions because of some very serious errors regarding the nature of man and God even before the fall. They claim that man was able to think and will independently of God even before the fall. They also deny the perfection of Adam since anything created must be finite and therefore imperfect. This is close to the Roman Church's scholastic teaching that the image of God in man is separate from the natural being of man. The image of God was added later to man (called in Latin, *"donum super additum"* or, an added gift). The fall simply caused man to lose this added gift, but the essential nature of man remained as it was before God gave this added gift. The result of both the Arminian error and the Roman error is that man can think good thoughts and make good choices even after the Fall, independent of the grace of God in Jesus Christ. In both of these errors we are able to see that it is not the Bible but heathen gnostic philosophy on which they rely – which teaches the basic evil of matter and the good of the spiritual.

Men have come up with some very imaginative lies in order to deny the totality of man's sin. Some have reinterpreted the Scripture so the Fall becomes only a myth. We can no longer rely on its historicity or reality. Others say that the Fall was a "good thing" for man because it allowed him to come to a realization of right and wrong. And, after all, if man had not fallen, God could not have shown his love in Christ. Or as Mormonism says, the Fall was good because it allows man to become as God! Still others say that the Fall is like catching a bad disease. Man is sick, but not unto death. All man needs to cure him is a "humanistic, holistic" approach – psychological, cultural, social, and educational advances.

With the dominance of the *theory of evolution*, the whole concept of "total depravity" is judged to be absurd. When you deny the Creator, the creation of man in the image of God, and the Fall, it is senseless to talk about sin or of salvation. Man is not depraved, he is just *deprived and under-developed*. With evolution the Fall of man is never considered, since evolutionists teach the reverse – man has risen! He started like an amoeba, progressed to the monkey stage and gradually developed into the complex being he now is. All it takes is a lot of time and a lot of mutations. Sin which man commits is not sin, but the result of primitive animal instincts which will change with time.

The evolutionist denies biblical revelation about both the creation and the Creator. With no Fall, there is no need for salvation or Christ. Without the perfect and absolute will of God, man can only rise to a level of acceptable societal averages. There is no standard of perfection for man since God and His law is denied.

The current false theology (not "theologies" since these are all different colored threads of the same piece of cloth) of "self-esteem," "positive thinking," "possibility thinking," Post-Modernism, and "New Age" cults have been waging a war against the teaching of total depravity. We are being told that the answer to all our troubles can be found by searching deeply within ourselves to find that latent goodness that is in all of us. One such popular self-esteem advocate, Rev. Robert Schuller, flatly states,

"I don't think anything has been done in the name of Christ and under the banner of Christianity that has proven more destructive to human personality and, hence, counterproductive to the evangelism enterprise than the often crude, uncouth, and unchristian strategy of attempting to make people aware of their lost and sinful condition." (*Christianity Today*, August 10, 1984, p. 24)

Again Rev. Schuller states, "What do I mean by sin? Answer: Any human condition or act that robs God of glory by stripping one of his children or their right to divine dignity." *(Self-Esteem, A New Reformation.* World Books, Waco, TX, 1982, p. 14)

Sin, when it is minimized, minimizes Christ and maximizes man. Rev. Schuller explains, "The most serious sin is the one that causes me to say, 'I am unworthy. For once a person believes he is an 'unworthy sinner', it is doubtful if he can really honestly accept the saving grace God offers in Jesus Christ." (*Ibid.* p. 98) So for those who follow the "self-esteem" theology which permeates so many Christian circles today, they must conclude as Rev. Schuller, *"Reformation theology failed to make clear that the core of sin is a lack of self-esteem." (Ibid.)* The Bible makes it clear that man's problem is an overabundance of self-esteem (I Jn. 2:15-17) and a lack of contrition.

It may be difficult to find an age in which the denial of total depravity and the exaltation of man's self-worth has been more openly propagated than today. These are extremely dangerous tools of Satan that feed the appetite of fallen man's pride. Over and over we are told that Jesus died for us because 'we were worth it.' However, to deny man's total sinful nature as stated in such passages of Scripture as Romans 3:10-19, 23, is also to deny that man's salvation is totally of grace. God saves us by grace and not because of any inherent good or worthiness in man (see Romans 5:6-8 and Eph. 2:8,9).

The unbeliever is attracted to a message that actually says that the subject of sin should be avoided since it is harmful for a person's self-image. It depresses and alienates people. It is too hostile toward our fellow man. Man is basically good – he just needs some guidance and encouragement. All that Christianity should do is bring him to this realization of the basic high value of the "self."

At the foundation of a host of ideas which repudiate the teaching of the total sinful nature of man is *denial*. It is not just his sin that he is denying, but God Himself. Remember what Romans 1:20 and 21 says, *"For since the creation of the world His invisible attributes are clearly seen, being understood by the things that are made, even His eternal power and Godhead, so that they are without excuse, because, **although they knew God, they did not glorify Him as God,** nor were thankful, but became futile in their thoughts, and their foolish hearts were darkened."* (Emphasis mine)

Given the totality of man's depraved nature, we can easily understand how and why he denies the extent of that sin. Therefore, all these errors are to be understood as a part of man's depravity. It is only a true understanding of the depth of man's sin which enables us to comprehend the sinful actions of men today – especially their rejection of the gospel. We hear the "New Age" theologians speak about the love and truth that is within all people. The ugly fact is that because of the fallen nature of man there is a great deal of *hatred* within us. By nature, man hates God and his neighbor (see Matt. 10:22; Jn. 15:18,19; 17:14; Rom. 3:10-12; 8:7; I Jn. 3:13,14; *Heidelberg Catechism* Q. 5).

It is sometimes said that "God hates sin, but He loves the sinner." If that were the case then He would send sin to hell and save the sinner. But he does not do this. Rather, the Scriptures warn us over and over that God will send judgment and cast all unbelievers into everlasting punishment. It is a vain and idealistic attempt by some to detach sin from the sinner – something only God can do.

Perhaps this is done to make God look better – more loving and compassionate. It actually makes Him look foolish, inconsistent, insincere, and unjust. II Peter 2:3-18 is a strong warning about the punishment that God will bring on unrepentant sinners. It is a *"fearful thing to fall into the hands of the living God"* (Heb. 10:31), who is a *"consuming fire"* (Heb. 12:29).

The trouble with these approaches is that if you do not come face to face with the seriousness of man's sin, how can you begin to speak of salvation? In proportion to the true and total depravity of sin will we see the true and total greatness of our salvation. The difference for man is like the difference of being healed from a bad disease and being brought back from the dead. To be consistent, the Arminian should also teach that Jesus did not actually have to die and rise again, but just get very, very sick, and be healed. They do not teach this, but the fact that Jesus had to actually die is due to the fact, and full proof, that His people were *dead* in their sins.

What Does the Record Show?

Let us briefly take a look at what is actually seen when we look deeply into man. Will we here find the worth, the ability, or the innate good that many insist is still part of the nature of man? If we look at man the way God does, notice what Romans 1:21-32 teaches about fallen mankind:

.".. *although they knew God, they did not glorify Him as God, nor were thankful, but became futile in their thoughts, and their foolish hearts were darkened. Professing to be wise, they became fools, and changed the glory of the incorruptible God into an image made like corruptible man – and birds and four-footed beasts and creeping things. Therefore God also gave them up to uncleanness, in the lusts of their hearts, to dishonor their bodies among themselves, who exchanged the truth of God for the lie, and worshiped and served the creature rather than the Creator, who is blessed forever. Amen. For this reason God gave them up to vile passions. For even their women exchanged the natural use for what is against nature. Likewise also the men, leaving the natural use of the woman, burned in their lust for one another, men with men committing what is shameful, and receiving in themselves the penalty of their error which was due. And even as they did not like to retain God in their knowledge, God gave them over to a debased mind, to do those things which are not fitting; being filled with all unrighteousness, sexual immorality, wickedness, covetousness, maliciousness; full of envy, murder, strife, deceit, evil-mindedness; they are whisperers, backbiters, haters of God, violent, proud, boasters, inventors of evil things, disobedient to*

parents, undiscerning, untrustworthy, unloving, unforgiving, unmerciful; who, knowing the righteous judgment of God, that those who practice such things are worthy of death, not only do the same but also approve of those who practice them."

It is difficult to interpret any of the above passage as depicting man's inherent good or self-worth. In Romans 3:9-18, Paul describes again the unrighteousness of both the Jew and Gentile alike. Here he says:

"What then? Are we better than they? Not at all. For we have previously charged both Jews and Greeks that they are all under sin. As it is written: There is none righteous, no, not one; there is none who understands; there is none who seeks after God. They have all gone out of the way; they have together become unprofitable; there is none who does good, no, not one. Their throat is an open tomb; with their tongues they have practiced deceit; The poison of asps is under their lips; Whose mouth is full of cursing and bitterness. Their feet are swift to shed blood; destruction and misery are in their ways; and the way of peace they have not known. There is no fear of God before their eyes."

Unless we disregard the Bible completely, we cannot escape the deadly fact and nature of sin. The very truth that men are denying the full reality of sin is itself proof of the depravity that blinds the minds of men. The Holy Scriptures teach us that man was created in the image of God, in perfect holiness, righteousness, and with a knowledge of God. After the Fall, while the image of God in man remained (see Gen. 9:6 and I Cor. 11:7), each of these parts of the image of God is now totally corrupted, depraved, perverted, and twisted so the real inclination of fallen man is to flee from God and establish his own sovereign rule.

After the fall, man was still man. He can be said to be a "free moral agent" in the sense that he can still make choices, but they will be completely self-centered. Man did not become a puppet, without any responsibility for his actions. He is responsible to God for them.

Regarding man's will the *Canons of Dort* teach: *"But as man by the fall did not cease to be a creature endowed with understanding and will, nor did sin which pervaded the whole race of mankind deprive him of the human nature, but brought upon him depravity and spiritual death; so also this grace of regeneration does not treat men as senseless stocks and blocks, nor take away their will and its properties, or do violence thereto; but it spiritually quickens, heals, corrects, and at the same time sweetly and powerfully bends it, that where carnal rebellion and resistance formerly prevailed, a ready and sincere spiritual obedience begins to reign; in which the true and spiritual restoration and freedom of our will consist."* (Third and Fourth Heads of Doctrine, Art. 16)

In the end, it can be said, *everyone will get just what they wanted.* The unbeliever, who hates God, wants to stay as far from God as possible. He will get his wish in hell. And the believer is not taken to heaven against his will, but he desires that perfect fellowship with God more than anything else. This is because the effect of regeneration is to give him a new will – one that believes the gospel, and seeks to glorify God. It is God working in us which causes us *"to will and do his good pleasure."* (Phil. 2:13)

A Deadly Serious Matter

The Reformed faith takes sin as seriously as the Scriptures describe it. Man is so dead that unless God breathes into him the breath of life (Jn. 3), he will continue in that present state of condemnation everlastingly! *"He who believes in Him is not condemned; but he who does not believe is condemned already, because he has not believed in the name of the only begotten Son of God. And this is the condemnation, that the light has come into the world, and men loved darkness rather than light, because their deeds were evil. For everyone practicing evil hates the light and does not come to the light, lest his deeds should be exposed. But he who does the truth comes to the light, that his deeds may be clearly seen, that they have been done in God."* (Jn. 3:18-21)

Some might object that in the Reformed church we talk about sin too much. I hope it is not too much, but I hope it is sufficient to tell unbelievers where they are without true faith – under the curse of God. And I hope it is sufficiently taught in order to acquaint believers with the sin and hell they have been redeemed from, so that they might truly be everlastingly thankful to God for His free gift. Our total depravity requires the totality of God's love in Jesus Christ. We say that all glory should go to God for our salvation. This can only happen if our entire salvation was really, totally the gracious work of our sovereign God.

QUESTIONS:

1. Explain why it is necessary to believe that regeneration takes place before faith.

2. In what sense can we say that if the Arminian is right, nobody will be saved?

3. Why do you think it is important and necessary to begin with the doctrine of total depravity in presenting the gospel to someone?

4. Give as many Scriptural descriptions as you can to picture man's sin (for example: blindness).

5. What is the error of saying that salvation is a cooperative venture where God provides it and man accepts it on his own?

6. What difference does it make if we accept the Arminian position regarding sin or follow the doctrine of total depravity?

7. What is the error in saying, "Man is free to choose salvation if he wants it," but "God's hands are tied if man does not act"?

8. In the light of what we have learned about total depravity, how must we answer those who hold to the theology of "self-esteem," etc? Show the error in these false systems of belief.

9. When we look at fallen man as described in the Bible (esp. Romans 1 and 3), what do we find? Give a list of the characteristics of man's sin as described in these passages.

10. Is man able to make choices with his will or is he a puppet with God pulling the strings?   Explain:

11. Explain what is meant when we say, "In the end everyone will get just what they wanted."

12. How is the "totality of our salvation" affected if we do not believe in the teaching of "total depravity"?

13. Why did Jesus actually have to die, and what does that have to do with the doctrine of total depravity?

6

The Doctrine of Total Depravity
Part 3

The doctrine of total depravity is not the invention of theologians meeting at the Synod of Dort, of John Calvin, nor of any man. It is the teaching of the Bible. It is extremely important that on this and other doctrines we have a good grasp of the passages which instruct us on particular matters. This doctrine of total depravity is taught in the Word of God.

Outline and Proofs from the Bible

The following scriptural proofs for the doctrine of total depravity are outlined under various headings, in general following the basic outline of *The Five Points of Calvinism* by David Steele and Curtis Thomas (Presbyterian and Reformed Publishing Co. Philadelphia, Pa, 1965). I have added to and changed their outline somewhat. The sheer weight of evidence should dispel all doubt.

1. "The wages of sin is death," not only spiritual, but also physical. This *spiritual death* took place at the moment that Adam and Eve ate the forbidden fruit.

> **Gen. 2:16, 17** *"And the LORD God commanded the man, saying, "Of every tree of the garden you may freely eat; but of the tree of the knowledge of good and evil you shall not eat, for in the day that you eat of it you shall surely die."*

Gen. 3:10, 11 *"So he said, "I heard Your voice in the garden, and I was afraid because I was naked; and I hid myself. And He said, Who told you that you were naked? Have you eaten from the tree of which I commanded you that you should not eat?"*

Rom. 5:19 *"For as by one man's disobedience many were made sinners, so also by one Man's obedience many will be made righteous."*

Rom. 6:23 *"For the wages of sin is death, but the gift of God is eternal life in Christ Jesus our Lord."*

2. Adam's sin brought *physical and spiritual death* on all his descendants as well as on himself.

Gen. 3:19-24 *"In the sweat of your face you shall eat bread till you return to the ground, for out of it you were taken; for dust you are, and to dust you shall return. And Adam called his wife's name Eve, because she was the mother of all living. Also for Adam and his wife the LORD God made tunics of skin, and clothed them. Then the LORD God said, Behold, the man has become like one of Us, to know good and evil. And now, lest he put out his hand and take also of the tree of life, and eat, and live forever – therefore the LORD God sent him out of the garden of Eden to till the ground from which he was taken. So He drove out the man; and He placed cherubim at the east of the garden of Eden, and a flaming sword which turned every way, to guard the way to the tree of life."*

Rom. 5:1, 12, 17 *"Therefore, having been justified by faith, we have peace with God through our Lord Jesus Christ. Therefore, just as through one man sin entered the world, and death through sin, and thus death spread to all men, because all sinned. For if by the one man's offense death reigned through the one, much more those who receive abundance of grace and of the gift of righteousness will reign in life through the One, Jesus Christ."*

I Cor. 15:21, 22 *"For since by man came death, by Man also came the resurrection of the dead. For as in Adam all die, even so in Christ all shall be made alive."*

Eph. 2:1- 3 *"And you He made alive, who were dead in trespasses and sins, in which you once walked according to the course of this world, according to the prince of the power of the air, the spirit who now works in the sons of disobedience, among whom also we all* *once conducted ourselves in the lusts of our flesh, fulfilling the desires of the flesh and of the mind, and were by nature children of wrath, just as the others."*

Col. 2:13 *"And you, being dead in your trespasses and the uncircumcision of your flesh, He has made alive together with Him, having forgiven you all trespasses,"*

3. As David confesses his own sin, he acknowledges that he as well as all other men are *conceived and born in sin.*

Ps. 51:5 *"Behold, I was brought forth in iniquity, And in sin my mother conceived me."*

Ps. 58:3 *"The wicked are estranged from the womb; They go astray as soon as they are born, speaking lies."*

4. The Scriptures conclude that because all men are born in sin and by nature are spiritually dead, they must be *renewed* – regenerated (born from above) – by the Spirit of God, before they can enter the kingdom of heaven.

Jn. 1:12, 13 *"But as many as received Him, to them He gave the right to become children of God, even to those who believe in His name: who were born, not of blood, nor of the will of the flesh, nor of the will of man, but of God."*

Jn. 3:5-7 *"Jesus answered, Most assuredly, I say to you, unless one is born of water and the Spirit, he cannot enter the kingdom of God. That which is born of the flesh is flesh, and that which is born of the Spirit is spirit. Do not marvel that I said to you, You must be born again."*

Jn. 6:44, 63-65 *"No one can come to Me unless the Father who sent Me draws him; and I will raise him up at the last day. It is the Spirit who gives life; the flesh profits nothing. The words that I speak to you are spirit, and they are life. But there are some of you who do not believe. For Jesus knew from the beginning who they were who did not believe, and who would betray Him. And He said, Therefore I have said to you that no one can come to Me unless it has been granted to him by My Father."*

Eph. 2:4, 5 *"But God, who is rich in mercy, because of His great love with which He loved us, even when we were dead in trespasses, made us alive together with Christ (by grace you have been saved)."*

I Pet. 4:6 *"For this reason the gospel was preached also to those who are dead, that they might be judged according to men in the flesh, but live according to God in the spirit."*

5. Because of the Fall, men are *blind and deaf to the spiritual truths* that may be presented to them. Their minds are darkened and their hearts wicked and depraved by their sin. Such corruption results in their being totally *unable and unwilling* to come to the truth on their own.

Gen. 6:5 *"Then the LORD saw that the wickedness of man was great in the earth, and that every intent of the thoughts of his heart was only evil continually."*

Gen. 8:21 *"And the LORD smelled a soothing aroma. Then the LORD said in His heart, "I will never again curse the ground for man's sake, although the imagination of man's heart is evil from his youth; nor will I again destroy every living thing as I have done."*

Eccl. 9:3 *"This is an evil in all that is done under the sun: that one thing happens to all. Truly the hearts of the sons of men are full of evil; madness is in their hearts while they live, and after that they go to the dead."*

Jer. 17:9 *"The heart is deceitful above all things, and desperately wicked; Who can know it?"*

Ezek. 36:26 *"I will give you a new heart and put a new spirit within you; I will take the heart of stone out of your flesh and give you a heart of flesh."*

Mark 7:21-23 *"For from within, out of the heart of men, proceed evil thoughts, adulteries, fornications, murders, thefts, covetousness, wickedness, deceit, licentiousness, an evil eye, blasphemy, pride, foolishness. All these evil things come from within and defile a man."*

John 3:19, 20 *"And this is the condemnation, that the light has come into the world, and men loved darkness rather than light, because their deeds were evil. For everyone practicing evil hates the light and does not come to the light, lest his deeds should be exposed."*

Rom. 3:10-19 *"As it is written: There is none righteous, no, not one; there is none who understands; there is none who seeks after God. They have all gone out of the way; they have together become* *unprofitable; there is none who does good, no, not one. Their throat is an open tomb; with their tongues they have practiced deceit; The poison of asps is under their lips; Whose mouth is full of cursing and bitterness. Their feet are swift to shed blood; destruction and misery are in their ways; and the way of peace they have not known. There is no fear of God before their eyes. Now we know that whatever the law says, it says to those who are under the law, that every mouth may be stopped, and all the world may become guilty before God."*

Rom. 8:7, 8 *"Because the carnal mind is enmity against God; for it is not subject to the law of God, nor indeed can be. So then, those who are in the flesh cannot please God."*

I Cor. 2:14 *"But the natural man does not receive the things of the Spirit of God, for they are foolishness to him; nor can he know them, because they are spiritually discerned."*

II Cor. 4:3, 4 *"But even if our gospel is veiled, it is veiled to those who are perishing, whose minds the god of this age has blinded, who do not believe, lest the light of the gospel of the glory of Christ, who is the image of God, should shine on them."*

Eph. 4:17-19 *"This I say, therefore, and testify in the Lord, that you should no longer walk as the rest of the Gentiles walk, in the futility of their mind, having their understanding darkened, being alienated from the life of God, because of the ignorance that is in them, because of the hardening of their heart; who, being past feeling, have given themselves over to licentiousness, to work all uncleanness with greediness."*

Eph. 5:8 *"For you were once darkness, but now you are light in the Lord. Walk as children of light."*

Titus 1:15, 16 *"To the pure all things are pure, but to those who are defiled and unbelieving nothing is pure; but even their mind and conscience are defiled. They profess to know God, but in works they deny Him, being abominable, disobedient, and disqualified for every good work."*

II Pet. 3:5 *"For this they willfully forget: that by the word of God the heavens were of old, and the earth standing out of water and in the water."*

6. By nature all people are *slaves to sin* and actually children of the Devil. Only by the regeneration (*ie.* by a new beginning or a new birth) of the Holy Spirit does this nature change.

Jn 8:34 *"Jesus answered them, "Most assuredly, I say to you, whoever commits sin is a slave of sin."*

Jn. 8:44 *"You are of your father the devil, and the desires of your father you want to do. He was a murderer from the beginning, and does not stand in the truth, because there is no truth in him. When he speaks a lie, he speaks from his own resources, for he is a liar and the father of it."*

Jn. 10:26 *"But you do not believe, because you are not of My sheep, as I said to you."*

Rom. 6:20 *"For when you were slaves of sin, you were free in regard to righteousness."*

Eph. 2:1, 2 *"And you He made alive, who were dead in trespasses and sins, in which you once walked according to the course of this world, according to the prince of the power of the air, the spirit who now works in the sons of disobedience."*

II Tim. 2:25, 26 *.".. in humility correcting those who are in opposition, if God perhaps will grant them repentance, so that they may know the truth, and that they may come to their senses and escape the snare of the devil, having been taken captive by him to do his will."*

Titus 3:3 *"For we ourselves were also once foolish, disobedient, deceived, serving various lusts and pleasures, living in malice and envy, hateful and hating one another."*

I Jn. 3:10 *"In this the children of God and the children of the devil are manifest: Whoever does not practice righteousness is not of God, nor is he who does not love his brother."*

I Jn. 5:19 *"We know that we are of God, and the whole world lies under the sway of the wicked one."*

7. Because the *reign of sin is over all men* and throughout the whole nature of man, all are under its power and therefore none is righteous in himself.

II Chron. 6:36a *"When they sin against You (for there is no one who does not sin)...."* (see also I Kings 8:46)

Job 15:14-16 *"What is man, that he could be pure? And he who is born of a woman, that he could be righteous? If God puts no trust in His saints, and the heavens are not pure in His sight, how much* *less man, who is abominable and filthy, Who drinks iniquity like water!"*

Ps. 130:3 *"If You, LORD, should mark iniquities, O Lord, who could stand?"*

Prov. 20:9 *"Who can say, I have made my heart clean, I am pure from my sin?"*

Eccl. 7:20 *"For there is not a just man on earth who does good and does not sin."*

Is. 53:6 *"All we like sheep have gone astray; we have turned, every one, to his own way; and the LORD has laid on Him the iniquity of us all."*

Is. 64:6 *"But we are all like an unclean thing, and all our righteousnesses are like filthy rags; we all fade as a leaf, and our iniquities, like the wind, have taken us away."*

Rom. 3:9-12, 23 *"What then? Are we better than they? Not at all. For we have previously charged both Jews and Greeks that they are all under sin. As it is written: There is none righteous, no, not one; there is none who understands; there is none who seeks after God. They have all gone out of the way; they have together become unprofitable; there is none who does good, no, not one. For all have sinned and fall short of the glory of God."*

James 3:2, 8 *"For we all stumble in many things. If anyone does not stumble in word, he is a perfect man, able also to bridle the whole body. But no man can tame the tongue. It is an unruly evil, full of deadly poison."*

I Jn. 1:8, 10 *"If we say that we have no sin, we deceive ourselves, and the truth is not in us. If we say that we have not sinned, we make Him a liar, and His word is not in us."*

8. The *final state of the wicked is hell*, which is clearly set forth to us in the Bible.

Matt. 5:29-30 *"And if your right eye causes you to sin, pluck it out and cast it from you; for it is more profitable for you that one of your members perish, than for your whole body to be cast into hell. And if your right hand causes you to sin, cut it off and cast it from you; for it is more profitable for you that one of your members perish, than for your whole body to be cast into hell."*

Matt. 7:19 *"Every tree that does not bear good fruit is cut down and thrown into the fire."*

Matt. 10:28 *"And do not fear those who kill the body but cannot kill the soul. But rather fear Him who is able to destroy both soul and body in hell."*

Matt. 11:21-24 *"Woe to you, Chorazin! Woe to you, Bethsaida! For if the mighty works which were done in you had been done in Tyre and Sidon, they would have repented long ago in sackcloth and ashes. But I say to you, it will be more tolerable for Tyre and Sidon in the day of judgment than for you. And you, Capernaum, who are exalted to heaven, will be brought down to Hades; for if the mighty works which were done in you had been done in Sodom, it would have remained until this day. But I say to you that it shall be more tolerable for the land of Sodom in the day of judgment than for you."*

Matt. 13:30, 41-42, 49-50 *"Let both grow together until the harvest, and at the time of harvest I will say to the reapers, First gather together the tares and bind them in bundles to burn them, but gather the wheat into my barn. The Son of Man will send out His angels, and they will gather out of His kingdom all things that offend, and those who practice lawlessness, and will cast them into the furnace of fire. There will be wailing and gnashing of teeth. So it will be at the end of the age. The angels will come forth, separate the wicked from among the just, and cast them into the furnace of fire. There will be wailing and gnashing of teeth."*

Matt. 18:8-9, 34 *"And if your hand or foot causes you to sin, cut it off and cast it from you. It is better for you to enter into life lame or maimed, rather than having two hands or two feet, to be cast into the everlasting fire. And if your eye causes you to sin, pluck it out and cast it from you. It is better for you to enter into life with one eye, rather than having two eyes, to be cast into hell fire. And his master was angry, and delivered him to the torturers until he should pay all that was due to him."*

Matt. 21:41 *"They said to Him, He will destroy those wicked men miserably, and lease his vineyard to other vinedressers who will render to him the fruits in their seasons."*

Matt. 24:51 *".. and will cut him in two and appoint him his portion with the hypocrites. There shall be weeping and gnashing of teeth."*

Matt. 25: 30, 32-33, 41 *"And cast the unprofitable servant into the outer darkness. There will be weeping and gnashing of teeth. All the nations will be gathered before Him, and He will separate them one from another, as a shepherd divides his sheep from the goats. And He will set the sheep on His right hand, but the goats on the left. Then He will also say to those on the left hand, Depart from Me, you cursed, into the everlasting fire prepared for the devil and his angels."*

II Thess. 2:8-12 *"And then the lawless one will be revealed, whom the Lord will consume with the breath of His mouth and destroy with the brightness of His coming. The coming of the lawless one is according to the working of Satan, with all power, signs, and lying wonders, and with all unrighteous deception among those who perish, because they did not receive the love of the truth, that they might be saved. And for this reason God will send them strong delusion, that they should believe the lie, that they all may be condemned who did not believe the truth but had pleasure in unrighteousness."*

II Pet. 2:4-9 *"For if God did not spare the angels who sinned, but cast them down to hell and delivered them into chains of darkness, to be reserved for judgment; and did not spare the ancient world, but saved Noah, one of eight people, a preacher of righteousness, bringing in the flood on the world of the ungodly; and turning the cities of Sodom and Gomorrah into ashes, condemned them to destruction, making them an example to those who afterward would live ungodly; and delivered righteous Lot, who was oppressed with the filthy conduct of the wicked (for that righteous man, dwelling among them, tormented his righteous soul from day to day by seeing and hearing their lawless deeds) – then the Lord knows how to deliver the godly out of temptations and to reserve the unjust under punishment for the day of judgment."*

II Pet. 3:7-13 *"But the heavens and the earth which now exist are kept in store by the same word, reserved for fire until the day of judgment and perdition of ungodly men. But, beloved, do not forget this one thing, that with the Lord one day is as a thousand years, and a thousand years as one day. The Lord is not slack concerning His promise, as some count slackness, but is longsuffering toward us, not willing that any should perish but that all should come to repentance. But the day of the Lord will come as a thief in the night, in which the heavens will pass away with a great noise, and the* *elements will melt with fervent heat; both the earth and the works that are in it will be burned up. Therefore, since all these things will be dissolved, what manner of persons ought you to be in holy conduct and godliness, looking for and hastening the coming of the day of God, because of which the heavens will be dissolved being on fire, and the elements will melt with fervent heat? Nevertheless we, according to His promise, look for new heavens and a new earth in which righteousness dwells."*

Jude 12-15 *"These are spots in your love feasts, while they feast with you without fear, serving only themselves; they are clouds without water, carried about by the winds; late autumn trees without fruit, twice dead, pulled up by the roots; raging waves of the sea, foaming up their own shame; wandering stars for whom is reserved the blackness of darkness forever. Now Enoch, the seventh from Adam, prophesied about these men also, saying, Behold, the Lord comes with ten thousands of His saints, to execute judgment on all, to convict all who are ungodly among them of all their ungodly deeds which they have committed in an ungodly way, and of all the harsh things which ungodly sinners have spoken against Him."*

Rev. 20:10-15 *"And the devil, who deceived them, was cast into the lake of fire and brimstone where the beast and the false prophet are. And they will be tormented day and night forever and ever. Then I saw a great white throne and Him who sat on it, from whose face the earth and the heaven fled away. And there was found no place for them. And I saw the dead, small and great, standing before God, and books were opened. And another book was opened, which is the Book of Life. And the dead were judged according to their works, by the things which were written in the books. The sea gave up the dead who were in it, and Death and Hades delivered up the dead who were in them. And they were judged, each one according to his works. Then Death and Hades were cast into the lake of fire. This is the second death. And anyone not found written in the Book of Life was cast into the lake of fire."*

9. Since all men are dead in sin and in bondage to Satan, they are *not able by themselves* to make any choice for good, or *to have true faith in Christ.* They cannot change their own natures or decide in favor of salvation. The sovereign Spirit of God alone can change the hearts of men.

Job 14:4 *"Who can bring a clean thing out of an unclean? No* one!"

Jer. 13:23 *"Can the Ethiopian change his skin or the leopard its spots? Then may you also do good who are accustomed to do evil."*

Matt. 7:16-18 *"You will know them by their fruits. Do men gather grapes from thornbushes or figs from thistles? Even so, every good tree bears good fruit, but a bad tree bears bad fruit. A good tree cannot bear bad fruit, nor can a bad tree bear good fruit."*

Jn. 6:44, 65 *"No one can come to Me unless the Father who sent Me draws him; and I will raise him up at the last day. And He said, Therefore I have said to you that no one can come to Me unless it has been granted to him by My Father."* (see Jn. 3:1-8)

Rom. 8:9-14 *"But you are not in the flesh but in the Spirit, if indeed the Spirit of God dwells in you. Now if anyone does not have the Spirit of Christ, he is not His. And if Christ is in you, the body is dead because of sin, but the Spirit is life because of righteousness. But if the Spirit of Him who raised Jesus from the dead dwells in you, He who raised Christ from the dead will also give life to your mortal bodies through His Spirit who dwells in you. Therefore, brethren, we are debtors – not to the flesh, to live according to the flesh. For if you live according to the flesh you will die; but if by the Spirit you put to death the deeds of the body, you will live. For as many as are led by the Spirit of God, these are sons of God."*

Rom. 11:35-36 *"Or who has first given to Him and it shall be repaid to him? For of Him and through Him and to Him are all things, to whom be glory forever. Amen."*

I Cor. 2:14 *"But the natural man does not receive the things of the Spirit of God, for they are foolishness to him; nor can he know them, because they are spiritually discerned."*

I Cor. 4:7 *"For who makes you differ from another? And what do you have that you did not receive? Now if you did indeed receive it, why do you glory as if you had not received it?"*

II Cor. 3:5 *"Not that we are sufficient of ourselves to think of anything as being from ourselves, but our sufficiency is from God."*

10. The *will of man is not free naturally*, but must be set free by God and, when liberated, is free to worship and serve Him. Man does not by nature have a free will, but, by the grace of God in Christ, has a

freed will.

Jn. 8:32-36 *"And you shall know the truth, and the truth shall make you free. They answered Him, We are Abraham's descendants, and have never been in bondage to anyone. How can you say, You will be made free? Jesus answered them, Most assuredly, I say to you, whoever commits sin is a slave of sin. And a slave does not abide in the house forever, but a son abides forever. Therefore if the Son makes you free, you shall be free indeed."*

Rom. 6:6-8 *"Knowing this, that our old man was crucified with Him, that the body of sin might be done away with, that we should no longer be slaves of sin. For he who has died has been freed from sin. Now if we died with Christ, we believe that we shall also live with Him."*

Rom. 6:18-22 *"And having been set free from sin, you became slaves of righteousness. I speak in human terms because of the weakness of your flesh. For just as you presented your members as slaves of uncleanness, and of lawlessness leading to more lawlessness, so now present your members as slaves of righteousness for holiness. For when you were slaves of sin, you were free in regard to righteousness. What fruit did you have then in the things of which you are now ashamed? For the end of those things is death. But now having been set free from sin, and having become slaves of God, you have your fruit to holiness, and the end, everlasting life."*

Gal. 4:31 *"So then, brethren, we are not children of the bondwoman but of the free."*

Gal. 5:1, 13 *" Stand fast therefore in the liberty by which Christ has made us free, and do not be entangled again with a yoke of bondage. For you, brethren, have been called to liberty; only do not use liberty as an opportunity for the flesh, but through love serve one another."*

Eph. 2:10 *"For we are His workmanship, created in Christ Jesus for good works, which God prepared beforehand that we should walk in them."*

Phil. 2:12-13 *"Therefore, my beloved, as you have always obeyed, not as in my presence only, but now much more in my absence, work out your own salvation with fear and trembling; for it is God who works in you both to will and to do for His good pleasure."*

I Pet. 2:16 *.".. as free, yet not using your liberty as a cloak for vice, but as servants of God."*

QUESTIONS:

1. From the Scripture verses in this lesson, choose <u>five</u> which you feel are most helpful in explaining the doctrine of total depravity to someone who has not heard of it. Write them down in the order you would use them and *explain why* you chose them.

2. Match the following:

1___ We inherit sin from Adam	A. I Cor. 2:14
2___ Naturally we are slaves of sin unto death	B. Rom. 6:23
3___ Only Christ can set us free from sin.	C. Jer. 17:9
4___ By nature we are "dead" in sin	D. Rom. 5:12
5___ We are conceived and born in sin	E. Eph. 4:18
6___ The gospel is foolishness to the unregenerate person.	F. Rom. 6:20
7___ None are righteous.	G. Phil. 2:13
8___ God causes us to will and do his good pleasure.	H. Eph. 2:1,5
9___ By nature men are alienated from God and blind in their hearts.	I. Rom. 3:10
10___ The wages of sin is death	J. Jn. 8:36
11___ The heart is deceitful & wicked	K. Ps. 51:5

7

The Doctrine of
Unconditional Election
Part 1

The second of the Five Points of Calvinism that we will examine is the doctrine of *unconditional election*. In the Canons of Dort this doctrine appears first, since it appeared first in the "Remonstrance" they were refuting.

There are some people who call themselves "Four Point Calvinists" because they will not accept this teaching (similarly, others have a problem with limited atonement). As we progress with this study it will be easy to see that one of these doctrines cannot be left out without destroying them all. They are dependent on each other and are welded together as the links of one chain because they have their unifying basis in the Bible. Those who claim to hold to only some of these doctrines will eventually have to admit that they hold to none of them as we have explained them here.

Those who have a difficult time believing this doctrine often say they just don't understand it. It may be for that reason, but more likely it is just a matter of not being able to accept it once it is understood. As with all teachings of Scripture, we must understand them with our minds, and accept them by faith in our hearts. True faith is not knowledge alone, but it must be grounded in sure knowledge, holding it to be true, and a hearty trust in what is taught in the Word of God.

It is important that we study this particular doctrine thoroughly, for many other doctrines are built on it. The doctrines of grace and the sovereignty of God cannot be honored without a firm grasp of the doctrine of unconditional election.

Based on Total Depravity

First, we must realize that the doctrine of unconditional election is wholly dependent upon a proper understanding of total depravity. We have seen from that study that man is in such a state of sin that he cannot and will not make any spiritual choice for good. He is simply unable by his own power to choose salvation in Christ. If God would have to rely on man to come to Jesus Christ none would or could be saved because man by nature is dead in sin. While some of fallen man's choices may appear good in our eyes, they can never be directed to the glory of God and can never bring him to salvation in Christ. The reason for this is that *good works must proceed out of true faith, be based on the Law of God, and be motivated by a desire to bring glory to God.* Good works cannot produce true faith, nor is true faith to be considered a good work of man. Left to ourselves we would still be trying to hide from God and hide our sins by our own inventions as Adam and Eve did.

It would have been perfectly just or right for God to leave all men in the state of sin and condemnation which they have earned by their inborn and actual sins. God would be just to condemn us all to hell, for, *"the wages of sin is death"* (Rom. 6:23) and *"all have sinned and come short of the glory of God"* (Rom. 3:23). God is never a debtor to man. He owes man nothing – man, whose whole being is corrupted and bent on rebelling against God all the time. How much more should we thank God for our salvation when we realize this!

How Then Can Man Be Saved?

If man cannot and will not choose to be saved and if he is totally undeserving of salvation, then how can he be saved? With men this is impossible, but with God nothing shall be impossible. The doctrine of unconditional election provides the first step to answer that question. If man is to be saved, *it must come as a work of God.*

Election

The word "election" means to "choose" or "call out." For example, God calls Israel his chosen or elect people because, of all the nations of the earth, God chose only Israel to be His covenant people in the Old Testament. *"For you are a holy people to the LORD your God; the LORD your God has chosen you to be a people for Himself, a special treasure above all the peoples on the face of the earth. The LORD did not set His love on you nor choose you because you were more in number than any other people, for you were the least of all peoples; but because the LORD loves you, and because He would keep the oath which He swore to your fathers, the LORD has brought you out with a mighty hand, and redeemed you from the house of bondage, from the hand of Pharaoh king of Egypt."* (Deut. 7:6-8) This explains clearly that it was not because Israel was bigger or better than any other nation, but they were chosen simply because of *God's sovereign love.* He had made a covenant already with their forefathers and He is carrying this out to their descendants.

The same may be said of Christians in the Church today. The root word for "church" in the Greek language (*"ekklesia"*) means "the called-out-ones." The Greek root for the word "church" is related to the word which we translate "elect" (in Greek, *"Eklectos"*).

Election is Unconditional

The term *"unconditional"* comes from the fact that there are no actions of man or conditions in man which obligate God to save him or to choose him to be saved. God alone sovereignly chooses who will be saved and who will not.

Arminianism does not debate the fact that God has "elected" people. Rather, they claim that God's election was based on the "condition" that man would first believe. It is the error of the Arminians here which ultimately leaves election unto salvation in the hands of men. God only provides the *possibility* of salvation to all, in hopes that it will be accepted by some. According to Arminian doctrine, some people, by their own free will, did choose salvation in Christ. God was able, before the foundation of the world to *foresee* which men would make that choice and therefore He elected them based on that condition – man's work of faith.

One of the clearest passages that teaches the "unconditional" character of God's election is found in Romans 9:10 - 14, *"And not only this, but when Rebecca also had conceived by one man, even by our father Isaac (for the children not yet being born, nor having done any good or evil, that the purpose of God according to election might stand, not of works but of Him who calls), it was said to her, The older shall serve the younger. As it is written, Jacob I have loved, but Esau I have hated. What shall we say then? Is there unrighteousness with God? Certainly not!"* Here, Paul is speaking about the election of Jacob over Esau. Before they were born or could possibly have done any works that merited God's choice, God chose Jacob and rejected Esau. The reason is stated, *"that the purpose of God according to election might stand, not of works but of Him who calls."* (v. 10) Does this make God unfair or unrighteous because He chose one over the other? Certainly not! See Romans 9:14, 16, 20, and 21. Unfairness would be a valid charge if man was deserving of salvation and didn't receive it, but that is not the case.

The Bible throughout teaches that God is the one who makes all the choices of what He will do. Nothing at all takes place unless God has, from eternity, ordained (predestinated) and caused it to occur. What God foreordains, He reveals in the course of history by His providential acts. All of history and man's acts are in the hands of our sovereign God. God's choice of man unto salvation is not based on some meritorious good that God can foresee in man, for this good does not exist.

Salvation, either in its *accomplishment* or in its *application*, is not by works which we have done or will do, but by the mercy and grace of God. Any merit on our part must be excluded, lest we begin to boast about our "choosing" or "accepting" Christ (see Eph. 2:9). Even our best works in this life are as *"filthy rags"* (Is. 64:6; see also Ps. 14:1-4) and defiled with sin. None could stand before a God whose purity and holiness is infinitely perfect.

One of the best definitions of the doctrine of unconditional election is found in the Canons of Dort, First Head of Doctrine, Article 7, where it states, *"Election is the unchangeable purpose of*

God, whereby, before the foundation of the world, He has out of mere grace, according to the sovereign good pleasure of His own will, chosen from the whole human race, which had fallen through their own fault from their primitive state of rectitude into sin and destruction, a certain number of persons to redemption in Christ, whom He from eternity appointed the Mediator and Head of the elect and the foundation of salvation."

Under the First Head of Doctrine, Article 9, the Canons of Dort state the "unconditional" aspect of God's election. *"This election was not founded upon foreseen faith and obedience of faith, holiness, or any other good quality or disposition in man, as the prerequisite, cause, or condition on which it depended; but men are chosen to faith and to the obedience of faith, holiness, etc. Therefore election is the fountain of every saving good, from which proceed faith, holiness, and the other gifts of salvation, and finally eternal life itself...."*

God could have chosen to *save all men* by His grace. He certainly had the power and the authority to do so. And God would have been just if He had chosen to *save none!* But, God did neither of these. Rather, He chose to save some and exclude others. He is under no obligation to save anyone. That is what the Bible reveals.

According to God's own Word, His election unto salvation is not based upon any *foreseen* act of good or some foreseen response of faith on the part of those He elected. If He had done this, salvation would no longer be by "grace alone." Man would have merited God's choice. The Scriptures make it clear that God acted by His own good pleasure and sovereign will when he chose to save His people.

Ephesians chapter 1 verses 4 and 5 are probably the clearest in teaching this. We read, *"just as He chose us in Him before the foundation of the world, that we should be holy and without blame before Him in love, having predestined us to adoption as sons by Jesus Christ to Himself, according to the good pleasure of His will,"* See also Eph. 1:9 and 11 on *God's purpose* and the matter of the *good* (sovereign) *pleasure* of God's will.

Because God is sovereign He can do anything He pleases. He is not bound by what *we might think is fair.* Man's sense of "fairness" is always defiled by his own sin and subsequent selfishness. God knows only perfect justice – and that demands that all men be condemned eternally to hell unless a perfect satisfaction for their sin is made to allow men to escape His wrath (see *Heidelberg Catechism* Q. 12). It should not surprise us that God does not save all men, but that He choose to save any!

Trinitarian Involvement

We must see the doctrine of election as involving the entire Trinity, even though we generally speak of God the Father as the one who elects His people. This doctrine must be studied in connection with the eternal covenant (or "council" which is the agreement made between the three members of the Godhead before the foundation of the world). While we do not have the revelation of this inter-trinitarian council as such, we clearly can see the results and the references made to it (*eg.* I Thess. 1:4-6; I Pet. 1:2;).

In regard to our salvation this is carried out in this manner: the *Father* chose out of all the world of lost sinners (whom He had ordained would fall through Adam) a definite number of people (His elect) that He would save (Eph. 1:4-6). It is also revealed that God had chosen *His Son* as the Mediator or Redeemer (see Hebrews 1:1-3; I Peter 2:6). The Father gave the elect to his Son that He might redeem them as His people. The Holy Spirit's task was the application of redemption for the comfort of every believer (Jn. 14:16-18; 16:7-15).

The Son, Jesus Christ, under the terms of this covenant did all that was necessary to save those who were chosen by the Father. This involved coming in human flesh, living in perfect obedience, laying down His life for the elect, and rising from the dead. We see that Christ is very conscious of His mission in behalf of those *"given to Him"* by His Father.

We see this in John 6:39,40 and chapter 10:17-18. We notice this especially in the High Priestly prayer of our Lord in John 17, particularly in verses 2-4, 6, 9, 11, 12, and 24: *"as You have given Him authority over all flesh, that He should give eternal life to as many as **You have given Him**. And this is eternal life, that they may know You, the only true God, and Jesus Christ whom You have sent.*

I have glorified You on the earth. I have finished the work which You have given Me to do. I have manifested Your name to the men **whom You have given Me** *out of the world. They were Yours,* **You gave them to Me**, *and they have kept Your word. I pray for them. I do not pray for the world but for* **those whom You have given Me**, *for they are Yours. Now I am no longer in the world, but these are in the world, and I come to You. Holy Father, keep through Your name* **those whom You have given Me**, *that they may be one as We are. While I was with them in the world, I kept them in Your name. Those* **whom You gave Me** *I have kept; and none of them is lost except the son of perdition, that the Scripture might be fulfilled. Father, I desire that they also* **whom You gave Me** *may be with Me where I am, that they may behold My glory which You have given Me; for You loved Me before the foundation of the world.* " (Emphasis mine)

The Holy Spirit's part in this covenant is to *apply* (by creating faith through regeneration and the preaching of the gospel) to the elect the salvation secured for the sinner by the Son, Jesus Christ. This application is made to the elect only, and not one of them is lost. Romans 8:11-17, speaks about the new life that the Holy Spirit breathes into God's people (see also Gal. 3:2,3,5).

The Spirit also brings us the comfort of the gospel and sanctifies us to walk in thankful, good works which God had before ordained that we should walk in them (Eph. 2:10).

Ephesians 1 speaks first about the election by God the Father (v. 4), the redemption of God the Son (v. 7) and then the sealing of the Holy Spirit in that salvation (vv. 13 14) See also II Cor. 1:22; I Jn. 3:9, 24; Rev. 7:3; 9:4.

I Peter 1:2 shows us the involvement of the whole Trinity in the matter of our salvation. Here Peter addresses the Church as: *"elect according to the foreknowledge of God the Father, in sanctification of the Spirit, for obedience and sprinkling of the blood of Jesus Christ: Grace to you and peace be multiplied."*

QUESTIONS:

1. Why is it impossible to say you are a "Four Point Calvinist" (*ie.* rejecting election or one of the other points of Calvinism)?

2. Knowing what we do about the doctrine of total depravity, why would nobody ever be "chosen" by God to be saved, if the Arminians are right about their teaching of election?

3. Why is it important to understand the doctrine of total depravity before we can properly understand the doctrine of Election?

4. How can God still be "just" if He chooses only to save some men out of the whole human race?

   • Would God be "just" if He chose to save none?
Explain:

5. What does the word "election" mean?

   • What other word is it related to?

6. What is the "condition" that the Arminians claim as the cause for God's election of some people?

   • If the Arminian is right about this, why would we have to say that salvation is no longer by grace alone?

7. What do we mean when we say that election unto salvation is "unconditional?" and, Give a Scripture verse that clearly teaches this.

8. Give two of the passages from Scripture that you think most clearly teach the doctrine of God's electing love?

9. Describe what each of the persons of the Trinity does in bringing about our salvation.

THE FATHER:

THE SON:

THE HOLY SPIRIT:

10. According to the passages quoted in this lesson from John 17, what does the Father do with those whom He has chosen?

8

The Doctrine of
Unconditional Election
Part 2

"Election is the unchangeable purpose of God, whereby, before the foundation of the world, He has out of mere grace, according to the sovereign good pleasure of His own will, chosen from the whole human race, which had fallen through their own fault from their primitive state of rectitude into sin and destruction, a certain number of persons to redemption in Christ, whom He from eternity appointed the Mediator and Head of the elect and the foundation of salvation. This elect number, though by nature neither better nor more deserving than others, but with them involved in one common misery, God has decreed to give to Christ to be saved by Him, and effectually to call and draw them to His communion by His Word and Spirit; to bestow upon them true faith, justification, and sanctification; and having powerfully preserved them in the fellowship of His Son, finally to glorify them for the demonstration of His mercy, and for the praise of the riches of His glorious grace." (Canons of Dort, First Head of Doctrine, Art. 7)

The Arminian View

The Arminian view of the doctrine of election is that God's choice of certain individuals unto salvation before the foundation of the world was based upon His *foreseeing* that they would respond to His call. He selected those only whom He knew would of themselves freely believe the gospel. Election therefore was determined by or *conditioned upon* what man would do. The faith which God foresaw and upon which He based His choice was not given to the sinner by God through His Holy Spirit since man is able to make this choice by his own free will, according to Arminian doctrine.

Thus, the sinner's choice of God, not God's choice of the sinner, is the final cause for his election. But how does the Arminian answer the words of Scripture like I Pet. 2:9 where it speaks of Christians as *"a chosen generation, a royal priesthood, a holy nation, His own special people, that you may proclaim the praises of Him who called you out of darkness into His marvelous light"*? or II Thess. 2:13 which says, *"But we are bound to give thanks to God always for you, brethren beloved by the Lord, because God from the beginning chose you for salvation through sanctification by the Spirit and belief in the truth."*?

The Canons of Dort, First Head of Doctrine, Article 9 states: *"This election was not founded upon foreseen faith and the obedience of faith, holiness, or any other good quality or disposition in man, as a prerequisite, cause or condition on which it depended; but men are chosen to faith and to the obedience of faith, holiness, etc."*) Again, Acts 13:48 says, *"And as many as had been appointed to eternal life believed."*

Errors Surrounding This Doctrine

There are various errors which emanate from Arminians and others in understanding this doctrine of unconditional election. Everyone is obligated to deal with the subject since it is so clearly taught throughout the Bible. Even the Arminian must admit that this teaching of election exists. But in order to be consistent with the teaching of free will, he is forced to say that man made the first choice and God only responded to it.

Another error that enters Arminian thought is that God elected *everyone*! It is left up to man to accept his election in Christ or reject it. This latter idea certainly destroys the meaning of the word "election." What is the point of mentioning it, if everyone gets chosen? What meaning does election have if everyone is elected? What this position does is give lip service to election while preserving the false idea that man still has the freedom to choose or reject it by the freedom of his own will.

The error in both of these teachings is that it allows God's plan of salvation to rest with sinful men. God is the servant of man's will. It is the sinner's choice of Christ that is the final determining factor of whether God will save him. The sovereignty of God and His grace is destroyed. While many believe that the cross is a gift of grace, they also maintain that man's coming to it in faith is man's own work. We must realize that basic to Arminianism is the firm belief that Christ died to give all men *an equal opportunity* to believe, and God must depend on man to respond to the offer.

The Fairness Question

The most common reaction against the doctrine of unconditional election is that it is *unfair to man and unjust of God*. What audacity to level such a charge against God! It is never within the sinful creature's jurisdiction to call into question the justice of God who alone does all things perfectly! We see here why it is so important to accept as a foundational fact the doctrine of the sovereignty of God. The simple fact is that if God had not graciously chosen some for salvation, *none* would be saved at all.

The fact that God did choose some, to the exclusion of others, is in no way unfair to those not chosen (called "reprobates"), unless, of course, we maintain that God was under some *obligation* to provide salvation for sinners. This is a position that contradicts the very meaning of "grace" as undeserved, unmerited favor. The Bible utterly rejects such a teaching.

We see this question raised in *Heidelberg Catechism* Q. 9 which reads: "Does not God, then, do injustice to man by requiring of him in His Law that which he cannot perform? No, for God so made man that he could perform it; but man, through the instigation of the devil, by willful disobedience deprived himself and all his posterity of this power." It is man, due to the Fall who has lost the ability to respond to the commands of God. It is not unfair for God to continue to keep the same demands for obedience as He did before the Fall.

Often coupled with the charge of "unfairness" is the accusation that those who believe in unconditional election are doing so out of pride. If that is ever the case it is a grave error. It is not a matter of pride for a Christian to express joy and thanksgiving in God's electing love. As a matter of fact, this doctrine is an expression of genuine humility on the part of a believer who has recognized his natural unwillingness and inability. Paul expresses this humility, *"But by the grace of God I am what I am, and His grace toward me was not in vain; but I labored more abundantly than they all, yet not I, but the grace of God which was with me."* (I Cor. 15:10)

Common Objections to Unconditional Election

It is said by some that the doctrine of election destroys the mission of the church since those that God has determined to save will be saved anyway. So, why preach the gospel or make an attempt to reach the lost? This is a false and ignorant argument (called Hyper-Calvinism). Admittedly, there are some who have held (or still hold) this position, and is even an accusation wrongly leveled against Calvinists. A Hyper-Calvinist would say that if the church gets too involved in missions and calls men to repent and believe, that this must be an indication that it is moving toward Arminianism. This is a serious error in understanding this doctrine, for it is *through the preaching of the gospel* that God gathers His Church. It is preached to all men so that, by the power of the Holy Spirit, God will gather His elect – His sheep. Question 54 of the *Heidelberg Catechism* also addresses this subject when it says the Holy Catholic Church: "the Son of God, by His Spirit and Word, gathers, defends, and preserves for Himself unto everlasting life a *chosen communion* in the unity of the true faith." See also Romans 10:13-17.

We should, however, be careful that the methodology of missions is consistent with the doctrines of total depravity and unconditional election. It is the duty of the Christian Church to proclaim and declare the gospel. It is to call, command, or *"compel"* (see Lk. 14:23) the lost to repent and believe in Jesus Christ. We are not to employ unscriptural methods that lure, snare, coerce, or trick people to make a decision. If we preach the gospel to all men, the Holy Spirit will work repentance and faith in the hearts of those who are ordained to eternal life, as Acts 13:48 says, *"as many as were ordained to eternal life believed."* Acts 16:14 says that Lydia, *"whose heart the Lord opened,"* listened and believed the words of the Apostle Paul.

When Paul wrote to the Corinthians he made it clear that the *success* of his mission to them did not rest with him. His purpose was singularly to preach *"Jesus Christ, and Him crucified."* Then Paul elaborates on that in saying, *"And my speech and my preaching were not with persuasive words of human wisdom, but in demonstration of the Spirit and of power, that your faith should not be in the wisdom of men but in the power of God."*(I Cor. 2:2,4,5)

One very popular approach to missions begins with the statement to all men, "God loves you, and has a wonderful plan for your life" (the first of the "Four Spiritual Laws" copyrighted by the Campus Crusade for Christ, Inc. 1965). This copyrighted method might sound good to the lost sinner, but can we say that it is true? Does God really love all men? If He truly did, He would have to do more than just offer them salvation, but He would actually have to save them all, since it is in His power to do so. And, if it is true that God loves all men, how can the Bible say, *"Jacob I have loved, but Esau I have hated"*? (Rom. 9:13) It is noteworthy that in these "Four Spiritual Laws" the Holy Spirit – the one who works faith in man's heart – is not mentioned until *after* the person has "received" Christ and is engaged in his "growth" in the Christian life. It would certainly not be wrong to say that the gospel reveals God's love in Jesus Christ, so that all who believe in Him will be saved.

The General and Effectual Call of the Gospel

The gospel must be preached to the ends of the earth, for the elect of God are spread throughout all the nations of the world. This extensive preaching of the gospel is called the "general" call of the gospel. This general call is "effectual" only to the sheep who are enabled to hear the voice of the Good Shepherd. John 6:65 says, *"no one can come unto me, unless it has been granted to him by my Father."*

Christ equates the *"elect"* with His *"sheep."* In John 10:26-28 Jesus explains why it is that the Jews rejected Him and others did not. He says, *"But you do not believe, because you are not of My sheep, as I said to you. My sheep hear My voice, and I know them, and they follow Me. And I give them eternal life, and they shall never perish; neither shall anyone snatch them out of My hand."* In the book of Acts, it is noteworthy that Luke comments on the Gentiles who believed the gospel, *"And when the Gentiles heard this, they were glad, and glorified the word of the Lord: and as many as were ordained to eternal life believed."* (Acts 13:48).

Again, notice what Paul says in I Cor. 1:18, *"For the message of the cross is foolishness to those who are perishing, but to us who are being saved it is the power of God."* (*cf.* also Rom. 1:16)

It is necessary that the *general call* of the gospel go to all the earth, so that God may work the *effectual call* in His elect people and save them. This is the Great Commission that is given to the Church by our Lord (Matt. 28:19-20).

Success Guaranteed and Comfort Given

Rather than being a hindrance to missions, this doctrine of unconditional election is a tremendous comfort. The comfort of the Reformed doctrine of evangelism is that it is *always successful* as long as the gospel is truly preached. We need to be careful that we define "success" in terms of the Bible and not in terms of the world. God will not fail to gather His Church – His called-out-ones. Paul, the great missionary of the Church, also says, *"How then shall they call on Him in whom they have not believed? And how shall they believe in Him of whom they have not heard? And how shall they hear without a preacher? And how shall they preach unless they are sent? As it is written: How beautiful are the feet of those who preach the gospel of peace, who bring glad tidings of good things!"* (Rom. 10:14-15) Then he goes on to say that *"faith comes by hearing, and hearing by the Word of God."* (Rom. 10:17; *cf.* also the NIV translation here) It is our task to go to the ends of the earth and preach the gospel to all men, for that is the very *method* that our Lord uses to gather His Church. Success does not depend on the numbers who respond to the call, but on whether we are faithful in the proclamation (see Joshua 1:7-9).

Since it is by the power of the Word and Spirit that God will gather His church, we can be sure that He will do it successfully.

The Lord Jesus explained to the Jews who rejected him that those whom the Father had given him (chosen) would be saved, and not one would be lost. Listen to His words, *"And Jesus said to them, I am the bread of life. He who comes to Me shall never hunger, and he who believes in Me shall never thirst. But I said to you that you have seen Me and yet do not believe.* ***All that the Father gives Me will come to Me,*** *and the one who comes to Me I will by no means cast out. For I have come down from heaven, not to do My own will, but the will of Him who sent Me. This is the will of the Father who sent Me,* ***that of all He has given Me I should lose nothing,*** *but should raise it up at the last day."* (Jn. 6:35-39 emphasis mine)

What a comfort is given to us in Romans 8:33 when Paul asks the question, *"Who shall bring a charge against God's elect?"* In other words, can man or the devil himself bring any charges against a man that causes him to lose his salvation? Certainly not. Paul answers the question with these words, *"It is God who justifies."* God is the one whose justice must be satisfied. And on the basis of man's faith in the atonement of Jesus, God's justice *is* satisfied. By grace through faith the believer is justified and has peace with God (Rom. 5:1). Since it is God who is offended by man's sin, and since it is God who provides the salvation in His own Son, and since God has accepted the work of Jesus as a perfect satisfaction for the sins of His people, no one can bring an additional charge against God's elect people.

Paul goes on in Romans 8:34 to ask, *"Who is he who condemns?"* Who can condemn the believer when it is Christ who has died, risen, ascended to the right hand of God, and makes intercession for His people? Christ is the Judge! If the Judge Himself has paid the penalty, who can condemn those for whom He died? What a wonderful assurance is given to the believer! Paul closes Romans 8 by saying that nothing whatsoever *"shall be able to separate us from the love of God which is in Christ Jesus our Lord."* (v. 39)

The success of missions does not depend on how many may believe the gospel. If that were the case, most of the great missionaries – even Jesus and Paul – would have been failures, for they did not get a huge following from their message. But both were sure of one thing, those whom God had given to Jesus through His eternal election would surely be saved. Not one sheep will be lost in the end. The Apostle Paul says in II Cor. 4, *"But even if our gospel is veiled, it is veiled to those who are perishing, whose minds the god of this age has blinded, who do not believe, lest the light of the gospel of the glory of Christ, who is the image of God, should shine on them. For we do not preach ourselves, but Christ Jesus the Lord, and ourselves your servants for Jesus' sake."* (II Cor. 4:3-5)

The Apostle Paul is careful to give God all the glory in his work when he says, *"So then neither he who plants is anything, nor he who waters, but God who gives the increase."* (I Cor. 3:7)

We should note also how Jesus sees the "success" of the preaching of the Word in his parable of the Sower (Matthew 13). God is accomplishing His eternal purpose throughout this parable. It is not an error or lack of success in the sower of the Word. Much of the seed sown did not take root, but that which fell on good ground bore a crop. It is the Holy Spirit who prepares the hearts of God's elect that the seed of the Word may have fertile ground and grow.

The work of missions does not ultimately depend on slick Madison Avenue methodology or the special wisdom of the preacher. Those who have departed from the Reformed doctrines of God's sovereignty have, sadly, resorted to the same approach to missions as the Arminians – often 'adding to the church those that are not saved' (*cf.* Acts 2:47) for the sake of the "growth" principle. Beware! says Paul in I Cor. 3:11-13, of the fire that will test the composition of all churches.

Rather than becoming lax in evangelism, the Reformed church should be in the forefront with gospel – gathering those whom God has given *"ears to hear."* The *biblical method* of missions is simply the *preaching of the gospel* to all men that the elect may be called out and separated from the world unto Christ by the power of God. The response to the gospel in Acts 2 was noted as: *"And the Lord added to the church daily those who were being saved."* (Acts 2:47b)

The most common characterization of the Calvinist is that of

"Hyper-Calvinist" (*ie.* beyond Calvinism). That is meant to infer that Calvinists do not preach the gospel sincerely, but only to those who they deem are the elect. This is ludicrous, yet admittedly there have been some who have characterized Calvinism in this way. We must reject that thinking since the number chosen by God is known only by Him. Further, it should be remembered that election is not salvation itself, but it is *election unto salvation.* God still uses His means of grace to bring about the fruits of election, namely, repentance and faith in Christ.

Likewise, we must avoid the error of presuming that all within the covenant (*ie.* children of believers) are elect unto salvation. One might just look at one such person – Esau – to see where this is not the case. On a larger scale we see that many of God's covenant people – Israel – were not believers. As a matter of fact the true believers were described as a *"remnant."* Paul addresses this matter in Romans 9:2-7.

Our covenant children are given the promises of the salvation if they repent and believe. And, should they die in infancy, or before making a confession of their faith, we have every reason to hope that they are saved. However, we should not be lax in the instruction or discipline of our children, with the *presumption* that they are elect unto salvation just because they have Christian parents.

The Matter of Human Responsibility

Another area of objection against the doctrine of unconditional election is in the matter of human responsibility. *Are men still responsible* for their actions since it is God who has determined who will and who will not be saved (sometimes called the "antinomy")? Do men have a responsibility to believe? Are they responsible for their actions, if God has ordained everything that will come to pass? The answer is *yes.* God commands all men everywhere to repent and believe in Jesus Christ. Those who do not, are judged in their unbelief. It is not just their unbelief that condemns them, but they *remain condemned* since that is the curse which abides on all unconverted men in Adam (see John 3:18, 36). God created man good and able to obey him, but with Adam's willful disobedience, all men are fallen into sin (see *Heidelberg Catechism* Q's 6 and 9). Fallen man does not reject the gospel against his will. This unbelief *is* the unregenerate man's will.

God in His sovereignty ordained that Judas Iscariot would betray Christ. This was ordained by God before the foundation of the world and was alluded to in the Old Testament in Psalm 41:9 and 55:12-14. Yet, he is held guilty for his action in the betrayal. Jesus said, *"The Son of Man goes as it is written of Him, but woe to that man by whom the Son of Man is betrayed! It would have been good for that man if he had not been born."* (Matt. 26:24) Judas felt the guilt for his actions, but he did not turn to the Lord, but uselessly to the Jewish chief priests to clear his conscience.

Likewise, the believer is held responsible for his actions. He believes, fully knowing what he is doing. The reason for this is that God has graciously given the Holy Spirit to work in the heart of the believer, so that when the Word of God comes to him, he understands it, accepts it as true, repents, and believes in Jesus Christ. This belief is man's will – not his fallen will, but his new, regenerated will.

He is held accountable for his life before God since God has given him this grace through His Holy Spirit. Phil 2:12 and 13 tell us that the believer must work out their own salvation with fear and trembling. The ability to do this is seen in verse 13: *"for it is God who works in you both to will and to do for His good pleasure."*

It is true that we cannot comprehend the mind of God in all these things. This gives us no right to ignore or reject either God's sovereign foreordination of all things or the responsibility of man to obey God in all things. Both are obviously taught in Scripture, and we must accept both. This difficult matter is called the "antinomy" since it *appears* to us that there are two laws contrary to one another. They might appear to be contradictory in our limited minds, yet they are surely not contradictory in the infinite mind of God who has revealed both His sovereign foreordination and human responsibility.

No one goes to heaven or to hell against their will. As mentioned earlier, *people get just what they want in the end.* The fallen man who rejects the gospel does so because he wants to. That is the state of his depraved heart. He does not love God or his neighbor. He will not repent and believe in Jesus. He has no desire to praise God now, much less forever in heaven. He will get just what he desires when he stands before the judgment seat of God.

God's elect people are not dragged into heaven against their will either. God has given his elect people a new will that desires to serve and praise God now and forever.

Reprobation

"What peculiarly tends to illustrate and recommend to us the eternal and unmerited grace of election is the express testimony of sacred Scripture that not all, but some only, are elected, while others are passed by in the eternal decree; whom God, out of His sovereign, most just, irreprehensible, and unchangeable good pleasure, has decreed to leave in the common misery into which they have willfully plunged themselves, and not to bestow upon them saving faith and the grace of conversion; but, permitting them in His just judgment to follow their own ways, at last, for the declaration of His justice, to condemn and punish them forever, not only on account of their unbelief, but also for all their other sins. This is the decree of reprobation, which by no means makes God the Author of sin (the very thought of which is blasphemy), but declares Him to be an awful, irreprehensible, and righteous Judge and Avenger thereof." (*Canons of Dort*, First Head of Doctrine, Article 15)

It follows from what has been said that there is also a doctrine called *reprobation*. This refers to the fact that there are those that God has not chosen, who are called "reprobates." Whether we say that God has *"passed by"* some or that He actually chose some to be reprobates has little distinction. The fact is that God has not chosen all men to be saved and has left some in their misery which they were born and have willingly placed themselves. Some people have insisted that we must call this "double predestination" since some were predestined to life and others to death. Because all things are determined by God, this is certainly true.

Paul speaks about this in II Cor. 13:5,6 where he says, *"Examine yourselves, as to whether you are in the faith; Test* (Greek - *"dokimazete"*) *yourselves. Do you not know yourselves, that Jesus Christ is in you? unless you are **disqualified**."* (*"adokimoi,"* from the same root word as *"test"*). *But I trust that you will know that we are not disqualified."* The Greek word translated by some as *"disqualified"* (KJV, "reprobate") is the word *"adokimos"* which literally means *"not standing up to the test," "disapproved"* or *"rejected."* In English, "probation" is a test given to man. So then, "Re-probation" is a *failure of the test.* Hence, we arrive at the noun "reprobate." It is always used in the passive sense in the New Testament.

In II Cor. 13:5, the *test* is whether Christ dwells in the people. In Titus 1:16 the test is the works of men, which when put to the test of faith, are "disqualified." Notice from the NKJV the various translations of this same word from the Greek: Hebrews 6:8 (*"rejected"*); Rom. 1:28 (*"debased"*); I Cor 9:27, Titus 1:16 (*"disqualified"*); II Tim. 3:8 (*"disapproved"*). The NKJV and the NIV have chosen not to use the word "reprobate," but in each case it refers to those who are lost.

Arminians have rejected the doctrine of unconditional election mainly because of the teaching of reprobation, because it does not seem "fair." It does not allow room for their teaching of the free will of man. Since God is loving, they say, God would not choose to have some of his creatures damned to hell. It is true that God is loving, but God is also a God of justice who does punish every sin, either in man or in the Son of Man (see *Heidelberg Catechism* Q's 11,12). His love and His justice are seen simultaneously as Jesus died (justice) on the cross as a substitute (love) for the elect.

No man has the inherent right to the gift of grace. The difficult thing for people to accept is that salvation is in God's sovereign control – He can save whomsoever He wills. He is not forced to bypass His justice in order to show His love. To say that if God has chosen some to salvation by grace, that then he is obligated to make the same gesture to all men is a denial of the concept of "grace" which is unmerited, unearned, undeserved favor. The Scriptures make this distinction clear in reference to Jacob and Esau. *"(for the children not yet being born, nor having done any good or evil, that the purpose of God according to election might stand, not of works but of Him who calls), it was said to her, The older shall serve the younger. As it is written, Jacob I have loved, but Esau I have hated. What shall we say then? Is there unrighteousness with God? Certainly not! For He says to Moses, I will have mercy on whomever I will have mercy, and I will have compassion on whomever I will have compassion."* (Rom.9:11-15, emphasis mine)

It is hard to see how the Arminian is not making the accusation of "unrighteousness" against God. By altering the clear teaching of the Bible and making salvation rest on the choice of man for the sake of making this doctrine more "fair," it seems that they are actually calling into question the "right" of God to act according to His own good pleasure. It would be far better to just let "God be God" and "man be man" as Scripture teaches us.

The Love of God

Arminian doctrine wants to maintain the rights and freedom of man and limit the right and freedom of God by using the concept of a *universal love of God*. This doctrine fails to answer the problem it raises. If election is based on God's foresight, why would God create those men whom He foreknew would not believe and thus be eternally lost? If it is true that God wishes all men to come to salvation, then why does He bring men into the world whom He is able to foresee will reject the gospel? In the end, the attempts to preserve man's autonomy and God's integrity does grave injustice to the security of man's salvation, and the sovereignty and grace of God. In the end such doctrine accomplishes nothing. The Arminian is left with the same problem he tried to avoid, and, at the same time, done an injustice to God.

A Doctrine of Comfort

Election, properly understood, is not problematic, but one of the greatest comforts a Christian can enjoy. To know that God has determined something means that neither man nor any other creature can undo it. The elect of God will not and cannot fall away (which will be more fully discussed in the doctrine of the perseverance of the saints).

It may appear that some have true faith and then later they lose it and even die as unbelievers, but the fact is, that they were not God's people from the beginning. Jesus notes this about Judas Iscariot. He had a lot of the outward markings of a true disciple, but Jesus knew that he had a devil, and he was lost (see Jn. 17:12). In the parable of the Sower Jesus points out that what appears to be faith may spring up in some, but it is not real faith, for it does not last. None of the sheep that our Lord sacrifices Himself for will be lost (see Jn. 6:37-39; 10:28,29; 17:24; 18:9). I John 2:19 addresses the question of those who have left the faith when it says, *"They went out from us, but they were not of us; for if they had been of us, they would have continued with us; but they went out that they might be made manifest, that none of them were of us."*

On the other hand, those who for a large part of their life might appear to be faithless may still be of the elect of God and come to repentance and faith by the work of the Holy Spirit in the eleventh hour (such as the thief on the cross). Who would have held out hope for the Apostle Paul before Christ confronted him on the road to Damascus? We may not make any final judgments on others, but we may judge by the fruits we see as to whether a person exhibits the fruits of true faith at a given time.

"The elect in due time, though in various degrees and in different measures, attain the assurance of their eternal and unchangeable election, not by inquisitively prying into the secret and deep things of God, but by observing in themselves with a spiritual joy and holy pleasure the infallible fruits of election pointed out in the Word of God – such as, a true faith in Christ, filial fear, a godly sorrow for sin, a hungering and thirsting after righteousness, etc." (*Canons of Dort*, First Head of Doctrine, Article 12)

The Arminian has no such comfort that God will keep that which He has sovereignly chosen since the choice to be one of God's children rests primarily with man. Once the doctrine of total depravity is seen from Scripture, the question of *"Then how can any man be saved?"* is answered in the doctrine of election.

The doctrine of unconditional election offers the greatest confidence and assurance for the Christian, and rightly so, for it is God's work from the beginning and it cannot fail. We should be concerned to understand and confess this doctrine of unconditional election simply because it is taught in the Bible. It also gives us the explanation of why some and not all men believe and are saved. It is not because of God's failure, but it is His triumph. Read Matthew 24:22-24 in the light of what the Bible says about the elect and the comfort God gives through it.

Finally, let us consider a problem that is raised in the minds of some regarding this doctrine. It is this: "If God only will save the elect, how can I know that I am one of the elect?" This should not cause doubt or confusion at all. On the contrary, if we truly are repentant and believe that Jesus has died for our sins, *that is the evidence that we are elected by God.* God works this faith only in the hearts of His chosen ones (remember Acts 13:48). Rather than cause doubt or questions, this wonderful doctrine of God assures us that our salvation, from beginning to end, is secure in the hands of the Almighty.

QUESTIONS:

1. Explain the Arminian doctrine of "conditional election."

2. How does the doctrine of unconditional election guarantee the success of the Church's mission work?

3. What is meant by the statement that "the *message* is the mission of the church"?

4. What is the error in saying to all men, "God loves you and has a wonderful plan for your life"?

5. What is the difference between the "general" and the "effectual" call of the gospel?

6. What is wrong with the thinking that if God has elected a people unto salvation, then we need not be concerned about evangelism since He will save the elect anyway?

7. When can we say the mission of the church is "successful"?

   • How does God define "success" in Joshua 1:7-8?

8. What is the error of "Hyper-Calvinism"?

- How does this error affect the mission of the Church?

- Can we sincerely preach the gospel to all men?   Explain:

9. Explain what is meant when we say that no one goes to heaven or to hell against his will.

10. What is meant by the word "reprobation"?

- Explain what is meant by "double predestination"?

11. What is the error in trying to deny unconditional election by claiming that God loves all men?

- In what way does this limit God?

- Explain why the Arminian is left with the same problem that he tried to avoid.

12. Why is the doctrine of unconditional election one of the most "comforting" ones in the Scriptures?

13. If unconditional election itself does not actually save anyone, but is only an election "unto salvation," why should we be so concerned that all Christians believe this doctrine?

14. Read Romans 9:11. How does this teach "unconditional election"?

- What does Romans 9:14-18 have to say about the matter of God's "fairness" or His "right" to save or reject anyone that He wills?

- If the Arminian is right about this, why would we have to say that salvation is no longer by grace alone?

9

The Doctrine of
Unconditional Election
Part 3

S ome opponents of this doctrine may wrongly receive the impression that there is a certain arrogance or conceit among those who believe in the doctrine of unconditional election. If that were true, it would be a sin. That certainly is not the purpose of this study which seeks only to defend the faith and reveal the teaching of Scripture on this subject. *"The secret things belong to the LORD our God, but those things which are revealed belong to us and to our children forever, that we may do all the words of this law."* (Deut. 29:29)

Rather than suggest any smugness, this doctrine ought to humble each of us to the dust. If any other impression is given, then we apologize for it. But we can and will not apologize for believing this doctrine which God has been pleased to reveal in His Word. We cannot depart from it, for therein rests the assurance and comfort of our salvation. If God has not elected a people unto salvation, then we are all eternally lost in our totally depraved state.

This doctrine is often called a "Reformed" doctrine. This is because some Reformed churches have consistently taught it. It is the faith of our fathers, but this is not a doctrine conjured up in ivory towers of Reformed academia. It is the unavoidable teaching of the

Bible. It is a great comfort to diligently search the Scriptures and see how God really does bring His redemptive will to pass. The number of references in Scripture to God's sovereign, electing love are overwhelming.

Outline and Proofs from the Bible

1. The Bible throughout teaches that *God has an elect people* whom He has predestined to salvation and eternal life. They are sometimes referred to as being "called" or "chosen".

> **Deut. 7:6-8** *"For you are a holy people to the LORD your God; the LORD your God has chosen you to be a people for Himself, a special treasure above all the peoples on the face of the earth. The LORD did not set His love on you nor choose you because you were more in number than any other people, for you were the least of all peoples; but because the LORD loves you, and because He would keep the oath which He swore to your fathers, the LORD has brought you out with a mighty hand, and redeemed you from the house of bondage, from the hand of Pharaoh king of Egypt."*

> **Deut. 10:14, 15** *"Indeed heaven and the highest heavens belong to the LORD your God, also the earth with all that is in it. The LORD delighted only in your fathers, to love them; and He chose their descendants after them, you above all peoples, as it is this day."*

> **Ps. 33:12** *"Blessed is the nation whose God is the LORD, And the people whom He has chosen as His own inheritance."*

> **Ps. 65:4** *"Blessed is the man whom You choose, And cause to approach You, That he may dwell in Your courts. We shall be satisfied with the goodness of Your house, Of Your holy temple."*

> **Ps. 106:5** *"That I may see the good of thy chosen, that I may rejoice in the gladness of thy nation, that I may glory with thine inheritance."*

> **Matt. 22:14** *"For many are called, but few are chosen."*

> **Matt. 24:22, 24, 31** *"And unless those days were shortened, no flesh would be saved; but for the elect's sake those days will be shortened. For false christs and false prophets will arise and show great signs and wonders, so as to deceive, if possible, even the elect. And He will send His angels with a great sound of a trumpet, and they will gather together His elect from the four winds, from one end of*

heaven to the other."

Luke 18:7 *"And shall God not avenge His own elect who cry out day and night to Him, though He bears long with them?"*

Rom. 8:28-30, 33 *"And we know that all things work together for good to those who love God, to those who are the called according to His purpose. For whom He foreknew, He also predestined to be conformed to the image of His Son, that He might be the firstborn among many brethren. Moreover whom He predestined, these He also called; whom He called, these He also justified; and whom He justified, these He also glorified. Who shall bring a charge against God's elect? It is God who justifies."*

Rom. 9:11 *"... (for the children not yet being born, nor having done any good or evil, that the purpose of God according to election might stand, not of works but of Him who calls)."*

Rom. 11:28-29 *"Concerning the gospel they are enemies for your sake, but concerning the election they are beloved for the sake of the fathers. For the gifts and the calling of God are irrevocable."*

Eph. 1:4-5 *"... just as He chose us in Him before the foundation of the world, that we should be holy and without blame before Him in love, having predestined us to adoption as sons by Jesus Christ to Himself, according to the good pleasure of His will."*

Col. 3:12 *"Therefore, as the elect of God, holy and beloved, put on tender mercies, kindness, humbleness of mind, meekness, longsuffering...."*

I Thess. 5:9 *"For God did not appoint us to wrath, but to obtain salvation through our Lord Jesus Christ."*

Titus 1:1 *"Paul, a servant of God and an apostle of Jesus Christ, according to the faith of God's elect and the acknowledgment of the truth which is according to godliness...."*

I Pet. 1:1, 2 *"Peter, an apostle of Jesus Christ, to the pilgrims of the Dispersion in Pontus, Galatia, Cappadocia, Asia, and Bithynia, elect according to the foreknowledge of God the Father, in sanctification of the Spirit, for obedience and sprinkling of the blood of Jesus Christ...."*

II Pet. 2:9 *"Then the Lord knows how to deliver the godly out of temptations and to reserve the unjust under punishment for the day of judgment...."*

Rev. 17:14 *"These will make war with the Lamb, and the Lamb will overcome them, for He is Lord of lords and King of kings; and those who are with Him are called, chosen, and faithful."*

See also *Heidelberg Catechism Q. 54.*

2. It was *before the creation of the world*, that God *chose a definite and limited number of individuals* unto salvation. He wrote these names in a book. His choice was not based upon any merit in man or any faith of man that God could foresee before creation. Election *is unconditional*. Man's faith did not determine God's election, but God's election determined man's faith.

3. God, not man, made this sovereign choice.

Mark 13:20 *"And unless the Lord had shortened those days, no flesh would be saved; but for the elect's sake, whom He chose, He shortened the days."*

I Thess. 1:4 *"... knowing, beloved brethren, your election by God."*

II Thess. 2:13 *"But we are bound to give thanks to God always for you, brethren beloved by the Lord, because God from the beginning chose you for salvation through sanctification by the Spirit and belief in the truth."*

4. God's election was an *eternal, sovereign decree*, made before time began.

Eph. 1:4a *"just as He chose us in Him before the foundation of the world...."*

II Tim. 1:9 *"... who has saved us and called us with a holy calling, not according to our works, but according to His own purpose and grace which was given to us in Christ Jesus before time began...."*

Rev. 13:8 *"And all who dwell on the earth will worship him, whose names have not been written in the Book of Life of the Lamb slain from the foundation of the world."*

Rev. 17:8b (referring to those NOT chosen) *"And those who dwell on the earth will marvel, whose names are not written in the Book of Life from the foundation of the world...."*

Rev. 21:27 *"But there shall by no means enter it anything that defiles, or causes an abomination or a lie, but only those who are written in the Lamb's Book of Life."*

See II Thess. 2:13 above.

5. The basis of God's *election was purely of sovereign grace.* God could foresee before creation who would believe, but that is not the basis for God's choosing anyone unto salvation. If something is of grace, then it cannot be by works.

> **Jn. 1:12-13** *"But as many as received Him, to them He gave the right to become children of God, even to those who believe in His name: who were born, not of blood, nor of the will of the flesh, nor of the will of man, but of God."*

> **Rom. 9:11** *"(for the children not yet being born, nor having done any good or evil, that the purpose of God according to election might stand, not of works but of Him who calls)."*

> **Rom. 9:16** *"So then it is not of him who wills, nor of him who runs, but of God who shows mercy."*

> **Rom. 11:5-6** *"Even so then, at this present time there is a remnant according to the election of grace. And if by grace, then it is no longer of works; otherwise grace is no longer grace. But if it is of works, it is no longer grace; otherwise work is no longer work."*

6. Good works are never the *cause* of God's election, but they are the *fruits* of His electing love. True faith in Jesus Christ and the works of thankfulness are the proof of man's election by God.

> **Matt. 7:17-18** *"Even so, every good tree bears good fruit, but a bad tree bears bad fruit. A good tree cannot bear bad fruit, nor can a bad tree bear good fruit."*

> **Jn. 15:16** *"You did not choose Me, but I chose you and appointed you that you should go and bear fruit, and that your fruit should remain, that whatever you ask the Father in My name He may give you."*

> **Eph. 1:11-12** *"...in whom also we have obtained an inheritance, being predestined according to the purpose of Him who works all things according to the counsel of His will, that we who first trusted in Christ should be to the praise of His glory."*

> **Eph. 2:10** *"For we are His workmanship, created in Christ Jesus for good works, which God prepared beforehand that we should walk in them."*

> **II Pet. 1:8-10** *"For if these things are yours and abound, you will*

be neither barren nor unfruitful in the knowledge of our Lord Jesus Christ. For he who lacks these things is shortsighted, even to blindness, and has forgotten that he was purged from his old sins. Therefore, brethren, be even more diligent to make your calling and election sure, for if you do these things you will never stumble."

Phil. 2:12-13 *"... Therefore, my beloved, as you have always obeyed, not as in my presence only, but now much more in my absence, work out your own salvation with fear and trembling; for it is God who works in you both to will and to do for His good pleasure."*

7. Those whom God chooses unto salvation will believe.

Acts 13:48 *"Now when the Gentiles heard this, they were glad and glorified the word of the Lord. And as many as had been appointed to eternal life believed."*

Phil. 1:29 *"For to you it has been granted on behalf of Christ, not only to believe in Him, but also to suffer for His sake."*

I Thess. 1:4-6 *"... knowing, beloved brethren, your election by God. For our gospel did not come to you in word only, but also in power, and in the Holy Spirit and in much assurance, as you know what kind of men we were among you for your sake. And you became followers of us and of the Lord, having received the word in much affliction, with joy of the Holy Spirit."*

II Thess.2:13-15 *"But we are bound to give thanks to God always for you, brethren beloved by the Lord, because God from the beginning chose you for salvation through sanctification by the Spirit and belief in the truth, to which He called you by our gospel, for the obtaining of the glory of our Lord Jesus Christ. Therefore, brethren, stand fast and hold the traditions which you were taught, whether by word or our epistle."*

II Tim. 2:10 *"Therefore I endure all things for the sake of the elect, that they also may obtain the salvation which is in Christ Jesus with eternal glory."*

James 2:5 *"Listen, my beloved brethren: Has God not chosen the poor of this world to be rich in faith and heirs of the kingdom which He promised to those who love Him?"*

8. The election of particular people unto salvation rests on the *absolute sovereign grace and power of God* who controls all aspects

of His creation. Apart from God's plan and power, nothing may take place.

Ex. 33:19b *"... I will make all My goodness pass before you, and I will proclaim the name of the LORD before you. I will be gracious to whom I will be gracious, and I will have compassion on whom I will have compassion."* (see also Romans 9:10-24)

Job 42:1,2 *"Then Job answered the LORD and said: I know that You can do everything, and that no purpose of Yours can be withheld from You."*

Psalm 115:3 *"But our God is in heaven; He does whatever He pleases."*

Is. 14:24, 26, 27 *"The LORD of hosts has sworn, saying, Surely, as I have thought, so it shall come to pass, and as I have purposed, so it shall stand: This is the purpose that is purposed against the whole earth, and this is the hand that is stretched out over all the nations. For the LORD of hosts has purposed, and who will annul it? His hand is stretched out, and who will turn it back?"*

Is. 45:12 *"I have made the earth, and created man on it. It was I – My hands – that stretched out the heavens, and all their host I have commanded."*

Is. 46:9-11 *"Remember the former things of old, for I am God, and there is no other; I am God, and there is none like Me, Declaring the end from the beginning, and from ancient times things that are not yet done, saying, My counsel shall stand, and I will do all My pleasure, calling a bird of prey from the east, the man who executes My counsel, from a far country. Indeed I have spoken it; I will also bring it to pass. I have purposed it; I will also do it."*

Is. 55:11 *"So shall My word be that goes forth from My mouth; it shall not return to Me void, but it shall accomplish what I please, and it shall prosper in the thing for which I sent it."*

Matt. 20:15 *"Is it not lawful for me to do what I wish with my own things? Or is your eye evil because I am good?"*

Rom. 9:21 *"Does not the potter have power over the clay, from the same lump to make one vessel for honor and another for dishonor?"*

Rom. 11:33-36 *"Oh, the depth of the riches both of the wisdom and knowledge of God! How unsearchable are His judgments and His ways past finding out! For who has known the mind of the Lord? Or*

> *who has become His counselor? Or who has first given to Him and it shall be repaid to him? For of Him and through Him and to Him are all things, to whom be glory forever. Amen."*

9. While God does foresee all things, the election of man unto salvation *does not rest on God's foresight* of what man himself would do with the gospel.

> **Rom. 8:29** *"For whom He foreknew, He also predestined to be conformed to the image of His Son, that He might be the firstborn among many brethren."*

Some comments should be made regarding this verse since the Arminians have used this word *"foreknew"* to establish their view of election as being based upon God's foresight of who would one day be faithful. He then chose those faithful ones to be His elect people.

It is true that God foresees man's faith. He foresees everything else as well. But it is *not true that God determines what He will do by what He foresees.* God does not elect unto salvation after first foreseeing how man likes the offer. After all, where does man's faith come from in the first place? The faith that God *"foresees"* is a faith that He Himself has brought about in man (see Jn. 3:3-8; 6:44, 45, 65; Eph. 2:8-10; Phil. 1:29; II Pet. 1:2).

God can only foresee that which He Himself has first determined to bring about. If God had to work faith in the hearts of men first, then He would have had to elect those that he gave the gift of faith. The premise of Arminianism falls, unless man can create faith by himself. This they erroneously hasten to agree with, maintaining that faith is the result of man's own free will. As we have already shown, man does not have the free will he claims he has.

A look at the grammar of this verse also helps explain it. We notice that the text says *"**whom** he foreknew"*. This means that election has already taken place since grammatically *"whom"* is the object of the verb, not the subject. It is the previously "elected" or the "predestined" people that God foreknew here.

The word *"foreknew" ("proegno")* does not appear often in the New Testament, but we should look at its root – *"to know."* This word has a broad meaning in the Scripture. It does not always mean to "recognize". It is most often used in the sense of "to love" or to "know with a peculiar interest, delight, affection, and action." See Gen. 18:19; Ex. 2:25; Ps. 1:6; 144:3; Jer. 1:5; Amos 3:2; Hosea 13:5; Matt. 7:23; Jn. 10:14; Acts 15:18; I Cor. 8:3; Gal. 4:9; II Tim. 2:19; and I Jn. 3:1.

It is most likely that the meaning used by Paul here in Romans is that of an "active divine delight" or "love." *God's love is the cause not the result of predestination* (I Jn. 4:10).

The basis for salvation emphasized in Scripture is not our "accepting" Christ, but *Christ making us "acceptable" to God* by His sacrifice (Eph. 1:6). The believers Paul is referring to here, as being *"foreseen in love"* (and also in Rom. 11:2), *have already been elected.* Paul is then singling out those whom God had elected to eternal life (as opposed to the reprobate whom God had passed by). So it is those that God had already elected in his love that He predestinates *"to be conformed to the image of his Son."*

We can see in the words of Paul that *it is God, not man, who predestinates, calls, justifies, and glorifies.* God is active and determinative in all these cases. This makes it inconsistent that in this use of the word *"foreknew"* man is active and God is passive. It is first God who sets His love upon His elect that He may do these things to men. To make *"foreknew"* to be based upon the necessity of man first having faith (as the Arminians do), is to break the chain that Paul here outlines – a chain whose links are forged, joined together, and strengthened by God alone.

This explanation of the word *"foreknew"* applies also where we find it in Rom. 11:2 (*"God has not cast away his people whom He foreknew."*) and I Pet. 1:2 (*"... elect according to the foreknowledge of God the Father..."*).

In any Bible study, if there is a word or a verse which is not clear and even appears on the surface to contradict other clearer teachings, we must compare Scripture with Scripture to determine its meaning in that context. We cannot ignore overwhelming evidence in favor of lesser evidence when we are questioning a difficult portion of the Bible. This comparison will give us a richer and fuller knowledge of the Bible. In the inscripturation of the Bible, God does not repeat Himself without purpose. There are many parallels in Scripture so that the Holy Spirit might work a greater knowledge and assurance of faith in His people as they are engaged in searching and studying it.

QUESTIONS

1. Why is it important that we see that this doctrine, and all others, comes from the Scriptures alone?

2. Write out one verse that clearly teaches that God does have an elect people that He has determined to save.

3. When did God choose those He has determined to save?

   • What Scripture verse clearly teaches this?

4. Good works are the _____, not the _____ of election.

5. Where has God kept a list of the names of those He has elected?

   • Where is this taught in the Bible?

6. How can a person know if he is one of the "elect" of God or not?

7. Match the following:

   1___ Man believes because God chose him.   A. Rom. 9:11-13

   2___ The names of the elect are written. . .   B. Matt. 24:22

   3___ God elected us before the world began.   C. Acts 13:48

   4___ Election was not because of man's works, but God's own purpose and grace.   D. II Tim. 2:10

                                                          E. Rom. 8:33

   5___ Good works confirm our

election.   F. II Tim. 1:9

6___ Election is unconditional
– not because God foresaw   G. I Cor. 16:8
good in man.

7___ Election is not salvation   H. Rev. 21:27
itself, but results in salvation.

8___ God will shorten suffering   I. II Pet. 1:5-11
for the sake of His elect.

9___ Nobody can bring any more   K. Eph. 1:4,5
charges against God's elect.

7. Give a brief explanation of why Romans 8:29 cannot support the idea that God elected people on the basis of His *foresight.*

10

The Doctrine of
Limited Atonement
Part 1

The doctrine of *limited atonement* follows closely and directly from the doctrine of unconditional election. God, who has chosen to save His people, will also provide this salvation in Jesus Christ.

The questions that are answered in this doctrine are these: "Did Christ die on the cross for every single human being, without distinction?" or, "Did His death have an actual, saving result only for the elect?" The first position – Universal Atonement – is that held by Arminianism; the latter – Limited Atonement – is held by the Calvinist. Only Scripture itself can answer these questions truthfully.

There are those who believe in a "Universal Atonement" in the sense that all men are actually saved in the end. That is not generally the teaching of Arminianism, but of modern NeoOrthodoxy. The type of "Universal Atonement" that the Arminian has adopted is that the atonement of Jesus was *intended* to be universal, but man's refusal to accept it by faith renders it *ineffective*. Therefore, the actual error of the Arminian doctrine is not universal salvation, but *the universal possibility of salvation*.

Atonement: Power or Possibility?

The real issue here is the power of the atonement of Christ. That is, "Does the death and resurrection of Christ *actually save*, or did Christ die just to make *salvation possible* for men (a possibility which man would be free to accept or reject)? The Reformed doctrine of limited atonement teaches that Jesus' sacrifice was powerful, and actually did save those whom the Father had given Him (those who were the subjects of God's electing love).

As we saw in the last lesson, election itself does not save – it only guarantees that salvation will come to the elect. *After election, the elect still stand in need of redemption.* This is accomplished by Christ in bearing the curse of sinners and being victorious over death. If the doctrine of unconditional election by God stands true as the Scriptures teach, then it must follow that God would not have the precious blood of His Son shed for those whom He has not chosen. Since they are not chosen, God knows that they will remain in condemnation.

What "Atonement" Means

"Atonement" means that man has been made *"at one" with God, that is, "reconciled" to God.* Since it was man's sin that caused enmity between God and man, sin must be removed if man is to be justified in the sight of God. This payment was made for the elect when Christ substituted Himself for us on the cross and paid the ransom for our sins.

The atonement flows completely out of the free and sovereign love of God (Jn. 3:16; Romans 3:24,25; I Jn. 4:9,10). God was under no obligation to save anyone. All that Christ accomplished in His suffering and death was because of the Father's love for His people (see Rom. 8:32).

The plan of God to save was purely out of the love and grace of God, without obligation. Yet, we must also see another aspect of salvation often referred to as the *"necessity of the atonement."* It was not necessary for God to save anyone, but once He has determined to save some, He can do it *only one way*. That way is through the death and resurrection of His only begotten Son. Only through this method of salvation can God be *"just and the justifier of the one who has faith in Jesus.*" (Romans 3:26).

The sin of man is an abomination in the sight of our infinitely holy God. God's perfect holiness and justice demands that sin committed against the Most High God be punished with extreme, that is, with everlasting punishment of body and soul (*Heidelberg Catechism* Q. 11). If God were to justify (that is, to declare someone righteous) in any way that did not involve the pouring out of His wrath against sin, God would have had to abandon His own perfect justice. In that sense only can we speak of the "necessity of the atonement" through the substitutionary, sacrificial, propitiatory offering of the blood of Jesus.

The Limited Nature of the Atonement

What was the "value" of the atonement? First, it must be seen that since Christ was both man and God in one person, the *value of His suffering and death was infinite*. I Peter 1:18,19 tells us that it was not with "*silver and gold*" but with the "*precious blood of Christ*" that we have been redeemed. If it had pleased God, the death of Christ could have resulted in the salvation of all men. That is, it was of *sufficient value* to save everyone, if God had intended to do that. Christ would not have had to suffer more if God had determined to save more. It would have taken no more of a sacrifice to save millions of people (or even all of mankind) than it would take to save only one person. God's perfect justice required that a perfect sacrifice of infinite value be made. Therefore, the number who are saved are not determined by the value of the sacrifice itself.

This matter of "the sufficiency of the atonement" is important since some would accuse Calvinists of limiting the value of Christ's death. The value of the blood of Jesus is not determined by the *number* it is applied to, but the *effect* that it brings to whom it is applied.

While the work of Christ was "sufficient" for all, it was *not efficient* for all. That is, its effect and intent would not be to save all, but only the intended subjects. Christ had no such intent when He died. He intended only to save those whom the Father had from eternity given to Him through His election (see how sharply Christ felt this as He prayed to His Father in John 17:2,3,6,9,12,24).

The reason why God did not elect all men and have Christ to die for all men remains a mystery to us, yet that is the teaching of Scripture regarding the plan of God. We certainly have no justification for thinking that God was obligated to save any or all men. If God were under obligation, salvation would no longer be by grace. What should be a greater mystery is how God could love even one person enough to choose him and send His Son to die for him!

If Christ would have died for all men and all men would come to salvation, then nothing would have been removed from the *power* of the atoning death of Christ. But it is clear from the Bible that all men are not believers and that many men are lost eternally. However, if as Arminians say, Christ died for all men, and yet some are lost, this must indicate that Christ's death *actually saved no one*. It would then have only provided the *possibility* or the offer of salvation. It would then be left for man to decide whether or not he will accept the plan of God and the work of Christ. This would put the *power of the atonement in the hands of sinful men*. If this is true and man rejects Christ's atonement, then God is rendered powerless to carry out His intentions. Christ's death would be good only if man decides he wants it.

It is easy to see, if Arminianism is right, that the whole of God's eternal plan is made dependent on man. If man is totally depraved as the Scriptures teach, and it rests with man by himself to repent and believe, nobody could or would be saved!

According to the Arminian doctrine of "unlimited" atonement, the blood of Christ was shed in vain for many. The fact, however, is that anyone whose sins are covered in the sight of God does not perish. *If Christ died for all, then all are saved* (a universal salvation that even most Arminians reject).

The Calvinist is often accused of limiting the power of the atonement by maintaining that it is effective only for some (the elect of God). But in reality, the Calvinist does not limit it – God limits it to *"His people"* (Matt. 1:21).

It is the Arminian who really places the limitation on the work of Christ when he limits *the power of Christ's blood and the power of*

God to save those whom He intended to save! The Calvinist confesses that God has limited the atonement *quantitatively* (with regard to the number), while the Arminian limits the atonement *qualitatively* (with regard to power and effectiveness). In this way they place a much more serious limitation on the work of Christ than they accuse the Calvinist of.

When we look at the work of Christ we must see it in terms of *reality and not possibility.* The atoning death of Christ actually accomplishes the only perfect fulfillment of the just demands of God – that the wages for sin be paid with death. The death of Christ blotted out both the curse which we have from Adam as well as our actual sins.

Just as the sin of Adam did not make the condemnation of men just a *possibility*, but it actually condemned us to eternal death, so the atonement of Christ did not just make salvation a possibility, but He *actually* secured salvation for those for whom He died.

To believe that God intended to bring salvation to all men, and in fact some are lost, is to say that God is not able to carry out His own will, or else He has later changed His mind. God is all-powerful and unchangeable. What He has determined to do He is both willing and able to perform. Listen to the powerful words of God through Isaiah, *"So shall My word be that goes forth from My mouth; it shall not return to Me void, but it shall accomplish what I please, and it shall prosper in the thing for which I sent it."* (Is. 55:11)

Mere man cannot overpower the will of the almighty, sovereign God, or foul up His plan by refusing to accept what God from eternity has willed! It is extreme arrogance to hold such a view. If some are lost, then this is the decree of God. It is not against His will, as if God had no control over that situation (see II Cor. 4:3,4; II Thess. 2:11,12).

The Arminian doctrine that attempts to vindicate God's "fairness" has made God a weakling whose hands are tied and only finite man can make the decision to untie them. Likewise it makes God a liar. God claims to be almighty, but if He is unable to perform what He wills (*ie.* saving all men, according to Arminianism), then God is, in fact, impotent.

The Lamb of God Died for His Sheep

Whom did Christ die for according to the Bible? He laid down his life for "*His sheep*" (Jn. 10:15,26-29). The Arminian would have to say that all men are Christ's "sheep" if He died for all. But, are they?

In Matthew 25:31-46 we read an account of the judgment day. What takes place there is important to understand. *Before* anything is said about the faith or the works of those judged, they are separated. The goats are on the left and the sheep are placed on the right. This "left" and "right" position is often used in Scripture to indicate who are lost and who are saved.

It is obvious that God knows from eternity who the goats are and who the sheep are. Those who are the sheep, and they alone, are saved. It was not by their works. Nothing is mentioned about works (including the "work of faith" which the Arminian assumes is man's gift to God) until *after* the separation. This was because the blood of Christ was shed for His sheep and the Holy Spirit had worked faith in their hearts. Not one sheep is lost in this process.

Jesus says in John 10:11 and 15 that He gave his life for the sheep. Now, if Arminianism is right and Christ died for all men, then all would have to be "sheep" according to John 10. And, if all men are "sheep", we would surely expect that there would only be sheep and no goats on the judgment day. That is, all men would be saved if all men are seen to be His sheep.

John 10 also speaks of those who are *not Christ's sheep* and, therefore, are not able to follow the Good Shepherd for they do not recognize the voice of Jesus. "*Jesus answered them, I told you, and you do not believe. The works that I do in My Father's name, they bear witness of Me. But you **do not believe, because you are not of My sheep**, as I said to you.*" (Jn. 10:25, 26).

The sheep are clearly given eternal life, not just a possibility of it – a possibility contingent upon how good their spiritual hearing is. "*My sheep hear My voice, and I know them, and they follow Me.*

And I give them eternal life, and they shall never perish; neither shall anyone snatch them out of My hand." (Jn. 10:27-28a) Could it be any clearer?

How does Christ *"know"* his sheep? John tells us that Jesus is very much aware that these were the ones "given" to Him by His Father. He knows those who were given to Him. See John 10:29 and 17:2, 6, 9, 11, 12, and 24. Those *"given to him"* He actually redeemed from sin and death.

The love which Christ showed in His death was not a general or indiscriminate love, but a very *particular love*. It was the love of Christ for His Church – His bride. If we say that Christ has a saving love and desire for all men, then Christ would be guilty of some sort of spiritual adultery – loving and marrying those who are not His bride. God's grace and love are never manifested as an indiscriminate shot-in-the-dark like Cupid's arrow, with the hope it will strike someone just right.

Is God's Justice Violated If the Atonement Is Limited?

I believe the motive for the Arminian here is to try to make God appear *more just* (an impossible mission!). While this may appear to be a noble gesture toward God and more palatable for man, since when does God need man to justify His actions?

Arminianism teaches that Christ died for all men. That's only fair, they say. But if Christ died for all men, then He also bore the curse and punishment of sin for all He died for. That is what the cross was all about. But, we know that all men are not saved – those who do not believe in Jesus are condemned to hell (Jn. 3:18,19). Even the Arminian (with the exception of some true universalists) admit to that.

If the Arminian is right, then God is terribly unfair. Christ would have suffered the penalty for sin on the cross (even for those who never believe), and then later God will pour out His wrath on them *again* in hell. This is two punishments for the same crime – double jeopardy. This is certainly not consistent with God's perfect justice. So, the attempt to make God appear more just results in making Him very unjust.

The salvation God gives us as a gift of His grace is *either total grace or it is not of grace at all*. Grace and works don't mix (Rom. 11:6). Loraine Boettner, in his book *The Reformed Doctrine of Predestination,* gives us the following fitting illustration. He says, the Calvinist has a narrow bridge (limited atonement) that goes all the way across the stream. The Arminian proposes that there is a wide bridge (unlimited atonement) that goes only half way across. For the Arminian to get to the other side, he will have to build the rest of the bridge himself by a work of acceptance in faith. This makes the work of Christ useless unless man adds his acceptance to it. This type of cooperative effort is foreign to the Scriptures. Man does not cooperate in the matter of his salvation, but he does "respond" to the working of God's Holy Spirit in his heart. The real "bridge" that God builds is narrow, but it does go all the way across!

Why All This Concern?

Why does the Calvinist get so upset about the Arminian doctrine of an "unlimited atonement"? It is not just for the sake of theological nit-picking or a good debate. This is a doctrine that strikes at the very heart of the work of Christ.

Arminianism reduces the cross to a mere wish – a gift laid before all men with only a wish that somebody will avail themselves of it. Where is the power of the cross? It is in the hands of man, and not in the hands of a sovereign God!

It may sound very benevolent to walk up to a stranger and tell him that "God loves him and Jesus died on the cross for him," and unless he accepts Christ in faith, that blood was shed for him in vain. But it's not true! Rather, we must tell all men that God sent His Son to bear the sins of His people so that those who repent and believe might have everlasting life. If they do this, then they will come to the fuller realization that God has not only chosen them, but Christ had them (their very names) in mind when He died on the cross. Once a person is a believer, he will both understand and believe in the love of God for His people (cf. I Jn. 4:15-16).

QUESTIONS:

1. According to the Bible, did Christ actually save anyone in His death, or only provide the possibility of salvation in His death? Give some proofs from the Bible.

2. If Christ did die for all people as Arminians say...

   A. How does that make God weak?

   B. How does that make God unjust?

3. What is meant by the "atonement"?

    • What is it that sets the "limits" on the atonement of Jesus?

    • For whom did Christ die?

4. (Fill in the blanks) God limits the _____ of the atonement of Jesus; the Arminian limits the _____ of the atonement of Jesus.

    • The sacrifice of Christ was "s_____" to satisfy for the sins of all men, but, according to God's plan, was "e_____" only for His elect people.

5. What teachings of John 10 support the doctrine of "Limited Atonement"?

6. In what way does the doctrine of a "Universal Atonement" deny the sovereignty of God and exalt the sovereignty of man?

7. What is wrong with telling all people, "God loves you, and has a wonderful plan for your life"?

11

The Doctrine of
Limited Atonement
Part 2

The Universal Benefit of the Cross

There is a sense in which all men, believers and unbelievers, have a benefit in the death of Christ. This is quite different from the universalism of the Arminian. For the unbeliever this benefit is *not a saving one*, and is only temporal. It is not a benefit that is based on merit. God is not showing kindness in hopes that all men might be persuaded to become Christians. Rather, it is a temporal benefit that comes to all men due to God's love for His elect people.

We have seen how this took place in the case of Joseph and the Egyptians. Gen. 39:5 says, *"So it was, from the time that he had made him overseer of his house and all that he had, that the LORD blessed the Egyptian's house for Joseph's sake; and the blessing of the LORD was on all that he had in the house and in the field."* (see also Gen. 30:27). The benefits of having Joseph around were obvious, yet it did not result in the eternal salvation of the Egyptians.

In Acts 14:17 we see that God causes the sun to shine and the rain to fall on the just and the unjust alike. While this may appear as a blessing to the unbeliever, it will ultimately be added to his curse since he will have to admit on the day of judgment that he used none of these gifts to glorify God. See Matt. 16:27; 25:24-46; Rom. 14:10-12; II Cor. 5:10; Rev. 22:12. The believer also receives these blessings and praises God for them.

For the sake of God's blessings to His people, the unbeliever may appear to prosper for a time. We may see this clearly in Psalm 73 (especially vv. 3, 12, 17-19, 27). In the end, the blessing for the believer is far greater – it is the nearness that he has with God (v. 28). For the sake of His elect and so that the gospel may go forth, God has ordained a certain stability and peace in the world which even the unbeliever partakes of. He may even receive some benefits from associations with the Lord's people. If sin were allowed to have free reign in this world, believers and unbelievers would be engaged in a full-blown physical battle as long as this world endures. There is enough persecution present already, but the true sinful heart of the unbeliever is not given free and total reign. Presently, the unbeliever is under restraint and even must obey some of God's commandments as the civil government may require or because it is acceptable behavior in a temporal society.

We should not confuse what is often called "common grace" to all men with the special "saving grace" of God shown only to his elect people. The benefits of Christ's work for His Church will be cut off for the reprobate and made even greater for the elect at the glorious return of Christ. John Calvin even speaks of grace before the Fall, in the sense that God was "gracious" to not place man in an unfinished creation, but had everything prepared as a Paradise before man was created. Man was placed into a creation that God had declared "very good."

Some have objected to the term used in theology of "common grace", because the non-elect should not be seen as receiving any grace at all. While he does not receive any grace that results in salvation or an easing of the wrath of God for his sin, yet what else would we call the gifts or talents that unbelievers possess? We use the term "grace" so as to distinguish this from the "work" of man. We are loath to give unregenerate man the credit for works which are his apart from God. If a heathen is able to develop some medicine that is of benefit to ease the pain or cure the disease of men, we should see this as a gift from God, rather than of man himself. God commonly uses the unbeliever to benefit His covenant people. Notice how Cyrus, an unbeliever, was used by God in the return of the Israelites to their land.

We likewise understand that these abilities or contributions of the unregenerate are not to be considered "good works" in the sight of God. Since they are works which do not proceed from true faith, are not done according to the Law of God, and are not done for God's glory, they are not good works. As a matter of fact all men will have to stand in judgment before God for how they have used the things God has given them – whether they are to His glory or not. See Romans 2:4-10.

There is then a benefit to all men as a result of the cross, yet it is not to be confused with saving grace or with a universal atonement for sin.

"Universalist" Passages in Scripture

We should look briefly at those Scripture texts which have been claimed by the Arminian to teach a universal "possibility" of salvation. In order to support a universal atonement, the Arminian usually relies on those verses of Scripture which appear to speak of Christ's dying for "all" men, or of the benefits of Christ's death for the "world."

We know that the Bible is God's Word – *inspired* (II Tim. 3:16 and II Pet. 1:21), *true* (Prov. 22:21; 30:5-6; I Thess. 2:13; James 1:18; I Jn. 2:21), and *unchanging and unchangeable* (Is. 40:8; Mark 13:31; Heb. 6:13-18; James 1:17; I Pet. 1: 23-25). Scripture does not lie or contradict itself because God, its author, does not lie or contradict Himself. When there are difficult passages that seem to say two different things, we must understand that only one doctrine can be true. We discover this by comparing Scripture with Scripture.

In the matter before us now, either Christ died for the sins of every single man in the world or He died for His people alone. Either He died to make salvation possible for all, or he died to make salvation a reality to some. But both teachings cannot be taught in the Bible since they contradict each other.

If we take a closer look at the passages that Arminians use to support their position, we must be sure to view them in their proper context. We must be careful not to "read another person's mail." There are words spoken and letters written in the Bible that cannot be used to apply universally to all men. For example, if we use Paul's letters, we must remember who he is writing to and what he is writing about. It is dangerous exegesis (or "isogesis") to just pull a verse out of a passage and build on it in isolation without realizing what the *context* is (*ie.* what the words around this passage are saying).

In the book of Ephesians, we cannot apply the passages of this book to all men universally. In 1:4 we cannot assume that *"he hath chosen us"* applies to all men. In 2:1 we cannot say that *"you hath he quickened who were dead"* applies to all men who may read these words. In 2:14 *"he (Jesus Christ) is our peace..."* does not refer to all men. And the list goes on and on. The basic clue to the proper interpretation of these and other passages is the fact that Eph. 1:1 states that this whole letter is written to *"the saints* (believers) *who are in Ephesus, and faithful in Christ Jesus."*

In I Corinthians 7 when Paul (being unmarried) is speaking about marriage he says, *"It is good for them* (unmarried and widows) *if they abide even as I."* (v.8) Is Paul teaching celibacy to all the unmarried? Is he saying that all missionaries or clergyman should remain unmarried? Certainly not, the context needs to be examined. He is speaking about himself, about the sanctity of marriage, and about being married at a time when severe persecution raged against the church. With regard to himself, it is better that Paul is not married since he is away much of the time in his travels and faces the danger of imprisonment. How could he be a good husband and father? In regard to the sanctity of marriage he says that it is better to marry than to be consumed with lust for a partner. And Paul is also speaking about the difficult times of testing for Christians. He is extending a warning to those who may be tempted to care more for their spouse than for the faith (vv. 23, 29-35). The context surrounding v.8 must determine how this verse is interpreted.

In a similar way, we must see the context of the so-called "universal" passages using the words *"all", "all men"*, and *"world."*

In the New Testament there was a constant need to address the false Jewish notion that they were the only ones God was determined to save. The New Testament writers correct this error by saying that Christ's death was intended for people of all nations, not just Israel. Christ died for all men *without distinction* (both Jews and Gentiles). But this does not mean that Christ died for all men *without exception*. The teachings, parables, and even the miracles of Jesus point to the fact that His saving work was intended to have a scope much larger than just Israel, but in no place do we read that Christ died to save all men. If he did, then His sacrifice was a failure.

The following texts speak of Christ's work being for the *"world."*

John 1:9, 29 *"That was the true Light which gives light to every man who comes into the world. The next day John saw Jesus coming toward him, and said, "Behold! The Lamb of God who takes away the sin of the world!"*

John 3:16, 17 *"For God so loved the world that He gave His only begotten Son, that whoever believes in Him should not perish but have everlasting life. For God did not send His Son into the world to condemn the world, but that the world through Him might be saved."*

John 4:42 *"Then they said to the woman, Now we believe, not because of what you said, for we have heard for ourselves and know that this is indeed the Christ, the Savior of the world."*

II Cor. 5:19 *"... that is, that God was in Christ reconciling the world to Himself, not imputing their trespasses to them, and has committed to us the word of reconciliation."*

I John 2:1, 2 *"My little children, these things I write to you, that you may not sin. And if anyone sins, we have an Advocate with the Father, Jesus Christ the righteous. And He Himself is the propitiation for our sins, and not for ours only but also for the whole world."*

I John 4:14 *"And we have seen and testify that the Father has sent the Son as Savior of the world."*

The following texts contain the word *"all"* in reference to the scope of Christ's work:

Romans 5:18 *"Therefore, as through one man's offense judgment came to all men, resulting in condemnation, even so through one Man's righteous act the free gift came to all men, resulting in justification of life."*

II Cor. 5:14, 15 *"For the love of Christ constrains us, because we judge thus: that if One died for all, then all died; and He died for all, that those who live should live no longer for themselves, but for Him who died for them and rose again."*

I Tim. 2:4-6 *"... who desires all men to be saved and to come to the knowledge of the truth. For there is one God and one Mediator between God and men, the Man Christ Jesus, who gave Himself a ransom for all, to be testified in due time."*

Hebrews 2:9 *"But we see Jesus, who was made a little lower than the angels, for the suffering of death crowned with glory and honor, that He, by the grace of God, might taste death for everyone."*

II Peter 3:9 *"The Lord is not slack concerning His promise, as some count slackness, but is longsuffering toward us, not willing that any should perish but that all should come to repentance."*

While at first glance these passages would appear to teach a universal atonement or at least a universal intention, yet in their context they clearly refer to the fact that *Christ died for men from all over the world, as opposed to just Israel* (John 3:16, etc.), for *all classes of men* (I Tim. 2:4,6), and for *all believers* (Heb. 2:9; II Pet. 3:9), but *never for every single human being*.

We confess that we believe in a *"Holy Catholic Church"* in the Apostle's Creed (see *Heidelberg Catechism* Q. 54). Some have replaced the word Catholic with the word "universal" to avoid confusion with the Roman Catholic Church. The word "catholic" refers to a church which encompasses believers from all over the world and throughout the history of the world. It is this sort of "universalism" that the Scripture refers to in the above passages.

Arminians cannot be true to their own position without saying more than they want to. If John 1:29 is taken universally (*"Behold! The Lamb of God who takes away the sin of world"*), then there would be no more sin in the world, or at least that every human being eventually would be saved. Actually, John the Baptist here is making reference to Isaiah 53 where in v. 8 Isaiah speaks of Christ being *"stricken"* for *"My people"* (a covenantal term used in regard to Israel). At that time, reference was primarily thought to be exclusively for the Jews. Therefore, John the Baptist does not say that Jesus came to lay down his life for the Jewish people alone, but for those who were Gentiles too. Therefore he uses the word *"world."*

In John 12:32 Jesus says, *"And I, if I am lifted up from the earth, will draw all peoples to Myself."* Did the Lord say that every individual in the human race would look to the cross of Christ for salvation? Certainly not. If he meant this, then it is obvious that Christ was wrong and his crucifixion a failure.

I Corinthians 15:22 tells us, *"... for as in Adam all die, even so in Christ all shall be made alive."* This passage is far from teaching universal salvation. It does tell us that since Adam represented all men – all died because of his sin. To say that in Christ *"all shall be made alive"* does not mean that Christ will make, or intended to make, every human being alive. Rather, this verse is universal as it applies to Adam, but limited as it refers to Christ. All men are, by nature, fallen in Adam. All who are *"in Christ"* (that is, are ingrafted into Him by true faith – see John 15:1-8) are given life. Adam is the head of the whole human race, and Christ is the head of His Body, the Church. All who are in Christ, were once in Adam; but, all who are in Adam are not in Christ.

For us, living in the twenty-first century, we must understand that the Jews of the first century had mistakenly assumed that only their nation would be saved by the coming of the Messiah, even though the Old Testament prophesied the day when the Church would extend into all the nations of the world (see Gen. 12:3; Psalm 72:8-10; Ps. 86:9; Ps. 87; Daniel 2:44; Zech. 8:23, etc.)

Acts 13:48 indicates that among the Gentiles, there was a faithful response to the gospel – *"those who were ordained to eternal life believed."* This was according to the plan and purpose of God. The atonement of Christ, in its scope and purpose, applied to both Jew and Gentile – to all who believed.

The context of every passage of Scripture is important. We

may not pick and choose certain verses that happen to say the words
we want them to, without taking Scripture as a whole. We may not
deduce any doctrine that clearly contradicts the predominant teaching
of the Bible elsewhere. Scripture must be compared with Scripture.
We must carefully determine the writer's purpose and audience when
God inspired him to pen those words.

Limited Atonement and the Mission of the Church

If it is true that God only intends to save his chosen people
and if Christ only died for them, then how can we bring the message
of the gospel to all men? And, if the elect are chosen to receive
salvation without fail, then why have a zeal for evangelism? They will
be saved somehow, someday, anyway. In the false view of "Hyper-
Calvinism," election and the sovereignty of God is stressed or
stretched to the point where the responsibility of man is reduced to
nearly nothing. We must avoid such an extreme and such error.

Can we *sincerely preach the gospel to all men*, knowing that
many of those who hear it throughout the world will never believe it?
It is inaccurate to say that we "offer" salvation to all men. The
preaching of the gospel is not an offer, but a "command" to repent and
believe in Jesus Christ. The non-elect person will never have ears to
hear this and obey. Yet, the call of the gospel must be sincerely given,
allowing God to gather his people by the power of His Holy Spirit.
Jesus explained His own ministry with these words: *"'And if anyone
hears My words and does not believe, I do not judge him; for I did not
come to judge the world but to save the world. He who rejects Me, and
does not receive My words, has that which judges him –* **the word that
I have spoken will judge him** *in the last day. For I have not spoken on
My own authority; but the Father who sent Me gave Me a command,
what I should say and what I should speak. And I know that His
command is everlasting life. Therefore, whatever I speak, just as the
Father has told Me, so I speak."* (Emphasis mine)

It would be a great error if we limited the preaching of the
gospel or mission of the Church because of this doctrine. Rather than
hindering evangelism, the doctrine of limited atonement enhances and
gives real meaning to preaching. While the messenger of Christ may
never say to all men indiscriminately, "Smile, God loves you" or

"Christ died for you," yet he must say that Christ died for the sins of His people and all men are commanded to repent and believe in Jesus Christ. Christ is the only sacrifice for sin and the only hope of salvation and everlasting life. It is likewise not wrong to sincerely command all who hear the gospel to "believe." It is precisely through this preaching of the gospel that God has determined to save His elect for whom Christ died (cf. Rom. 10:14-18). We cannot determine who the elect are, so as to skip some in the spread of the gospel.

God will also use the preaching of the gospel to condemn those who reject it and continue in their unbelief. See *Heidelberg Catechism* Q. 84 on preaching as one of the keys to the kingdom of God. The unbeliever remains in the state of condemnation (John 3:18; Jude v. 8).

The *success of preaching is guaranteed*, for none of the sheep will be lost (Jn. 6:37,39). Faith comes by the hearing of the Word of God (Rom. 10:17). Those who hear the voice of the Good Shepherd, who speaks through His Word, will, by the power of the Holy Spirit, recognize His voice and will follow Jesus because they are His sheep (John 10:27). Others do not hear the voice of Jesus and will not believe, because they are not His sheep whom He died for (John 10:26).

The preacher does not have to rely (indeed, it would be wrong to) on his own cunningness, slick words, emotional appeal, or entertainment in order to get a response of faith from the sinner. See I Cor. 2:1-8. The only method which the Bible outlines for doing mission work is to *go* to all men and *preach the gospel*. God will apply the message to the hearts of His elect through the regenerating work of the Holy Spirit. It is the duty of the preacher and of all believers to *pray for all men that they might believe the gospel* with the realization that the sheep surely will believe. It is the Christian's duty to sow the seed of the Word and God will bring the increase.

The decree of election determines for whom Christ would lay down his life. This decree is a sacred decree. We as mere men do not know whom God has chosen, but only that those chosen will be repent, believe, and be saved. Therefore, we can be assured of success in missions. Success is not determined by how many become

Christians, but it is a matter of *faithfulness in bringing the true gospel* of salvation to the ends of the earth. God tells Joshua that if he is faithful to the Word of God he will have success (Joshua 1:8).

We are commanded to preach the gospel to all men. The results of preaching lie in God's hand, not in man's. We are responsible to maintain the purity of doctrine and bring it to men. Unfortunately, in a mistaken attempt to bring all men into the Church, men have forsaken true doctrine in order to give greater appeal to the sound of the gospel. It may sound like a nice way to approach all men and say "Christ died for you, now you must choose Him," but it is not true, and does grave injustice to the intent of Christ on the cross. The apostle Paul understood this when he said that he did not use *"persuasive words of human wisdom, but in demonstration of the Spirit and of power, that your faith should not be in the wisdom of men but in the power of God."* (I Cor. 2:4, 5)

Knowing that God will not save all men, how shall we preach the message of the gospel? The answer may first be seen in the ministry of Christ, or Peter or Paul. They preached the same message to all. Some believed and some did not. When we say that we "freely proclaim" the gospel we must not think that all men are equally capable of receiving it in faith. The unregenerate man is not "free" to believe – not until and unless the Holy Spirit has brought new life and freedom into his heart. No man can do this himself. Only the sheep will listen, and that will be only because the Holy Spirit works faith in their hearts.

It should be remembered the purpose of preaching the gospel is two-fold. It is a message of salvation to all who believe, and a message condemnation to all who reject it. But all men need to hear it.

Is it a "sincere" message if we know some will reject it because their hearts will remain hardened? Yes. The sincerity of the message proclaimed is not dependent on its results. Notice the sincerity of Jesus in Matthew 23:37 when he says, *"O Jerusalem, Jerusalem, the one who kills the prophets and stones those who are sent to her! How often I wanted to gather your children together, as a hen gathers her chicks under her wings, but you were not willing!"*

Sincerely we must say, "Jesus died on the cross for the sins of His people that all who believe in Him might have life everlasting. You must repent and believe in him for salvation. If you do not you remain lost." We must pray sincerely and earnestly that God will apply His truth to the hearts of His people that they may be saved. We sincerely confess that God will gather His Church through the preaching of Christ crucified, risen, and reigning.

If zeal for missions is dampened in any way by the doctrines of election and limited atonement, then we have misunderstood them and should go back to the Scriptures and study them again.

In the realm of theology there are perhaps no more ridiculed doctrines than that of God's unconditional election and the limited atonement of Christ. To many people this is just an example of fanatical narrow-mindedness – unfair, false and foolish. But these doctrines are the true teachings of Scripture in which we rejoice and upon which we are not ashamed to stand.

QUESTIONS:

1. What is meant by "universalistic" passages of Scripture?

● What words are "universalistic" words, and give examples of what these mean in their context?

2. What principles of interpretation must be followed when there are verses that seem to us to contradict each other?

● What is meant by "reading other people's mail" in reference to interpreting Scripture?

3. In what sense can we say that the death of Christ has a temporal benefit for all men?

● What sort of "grace" is this?

● What are some of these benefits?

4. Give some examples from the Bible where unbelievers enjoyed God's blessing due to the fact that God was actually blessing His people?

5. Why is it improper for us to say to all men, "Smile, God loves you"? or "God loves you, and has a wonderful plan for your life"?

  • What do we mean when we say that God is a God of love, or that "God is love?"

6. In view of the doctrine of "Limited Atonement," what must we say to all men in bringing them the gospel?

  • Explain why this doctrine does not hinder the "sincere" presentation of the gospel to all men.

7. If God is going to save His elect people anyway, why should we be concerned to obey the Great Commission to go to all the world and preach the gospel?

  • What two-fold message is there in all true preaching of the gospel and why is this called a *key* to the Kingdom of God?

12

The Doctrine of
Limited Atonement
Part 3

Outline and Proofs from the Bible

The overwhelming evidence from Scripture is that Christ came to save a very *definite number of people* (those *given to him* by the Father). In this regard, see the following texts:

Matt. 1:21 *"And she will bring forth a Son, and you shall call His name Jesus, for He will save His people from their sins."*

Matt. 20:28 *"... just as the Son of Man did not come to be served, but to serve, and to give His life a ransom for many."*

Matt. 26:28 *"For this is My blood of the new covenant, which is shed for many for the remission of sins."*

John 10:11, 15 *"I am the good shepherd. The good shepherd gives His life for the sheep. As the Father knows Me, even so I know the Father; and I lay down My life for the sheep."*

Acts 13:48 *"Now when the Gentiles heard this, they were glad and glorified the word of the Lord. And as many as had been appointed to eternal life believed."*

Acts 20:28 *"Therefore take heed to yourselves and to all the flock, among which the Holy Spirit has made you overseers, to shepherd* *the church of God which He purchased with His own blood."*

Rom. 8:32-34 *"He who did not spare His own Son, but delivered Him up for us all, how shall He not with Him also freely give us all things? Who shall bring a charge against God's elect? It is God who justifies. Who is he who condemns? It is Christ who died, and furthermore is also risen, who is even at the right hand of God, who also makes intercession for us."*

Eph. 5:25-27 *"Husbands, love your wives, just as Christ also loved the church and gave Himself for it, that He might sanctify and cleanse it with the washing of water by the word, that He might present it to Himself a glorious church, not having spot or wrinkle or any such thing, but that it should be holy and without blemish."*

Heb. 2:17 *"Therefore, in all things He had to be made like His brethren, that He might be a merciful and faithful High Priest in things pertaining to God, to make propitiation for the sins of the people."*

Heb. 9:15, 28 *"And for this reason He is the Mediator of the new covenant, by means of death, for the redemption of the transgressions under the first covenant, that those who are called may receive the promise of the eternal inheritance. So Christ was offered once to bear the sins of many. To those who eagerly wait for Him He will appear a second time, apart from sin, for salvation."*

Rev. 5:9 *"And they sang a new song, saying: You are worthy to take the scroll, and to open its seals; for You were slain, and have redeemed us to God by Your blood out of every tribe and tongue and people and nation."*

The following survey may help you in tracing the purpose and scope of Christ's saving work.

1. The Bible describes the purpose of *Christ's work as the full salvation of his people* (that is, actual salvation, not just the possibility of it):

● The Bible tells us that *Christ came to actually save sinners*, not to allow the success of His work to be determined by sinners.

Matt. 1:21 *"And she will bring forth a Son, and you shall call His name Jesus, for He will save His people from their sins."*

Luke 19:10 *"for the Son of Man has come to seek and to save that* *which was lost."*

II Cor. 5:21 *"For He made Him who knew no sin to be sin for us, that we might become the righteousness of God in Him."*

I Peter 3:18 *"For Christ also suffered once for sins, the just for the unjust, that He might bring us to God, being put to death in the flesh but made alive by the Spirit."*

Gal. 1:3-4 *"Grace to you and peace from God the Father and our Lord Jesus Christ, who gave Himself for our sins, that He might deliver us from this present evil age, according to the will of our God and Father."*

I Tim. 1:15 *"This is a faithful saying and worthy of all acceptance, that Christ Jesus came into the world to save sinners, of whom I am chief."*

Titus 2:14 *"... who gave Himself for us, that He might redeem us from every lawless deed and purify for Himself His own special people, zealous for good works."*

• **The death of Christ actually reconciles sinners to God** (remember that in each of these passages the author is writing to the Church of true believers).

Romans 5:10 *"For if when we were enemies we were reconciled to God through the death of His Son, much more, having been reconciled, we shall be saved by His life."*

II Cor. 5:18-21 *"Now all things are of God, who has reconciled us to Himself through Jesus Christ, and has given us the ministry of reconciliation, that is, that God was in Christ reconciling the world to Himself, not imputing their trespasses to them, and has committed to us the word of reconciliation. Therefore we are ambassadors for Christ, as though God were pleading through us: we implore you on Christ's behalf, be reconciled to God. For He made Him who knew no sin to be sin for us, that we might become the righteousness of God in Him."*

Eph. 2:15-18 *"having abolished in His flesh the enmity, that is, the law of commandments contained in ordinances, so as to create in Himself one new man from the two, thus making peace, and that He might reconcile them both to God in one body through the cross, thereby putting to death the enmity. And He came and preached peace to you who were afar off and to those who were near. For* *through Him we both have access by one Spirit to the Father."*

Col. 1:20-22 *"And by Him to reconcile all things to Himself, by Him, whether things on earth or things in heaven, having made peace through the blood of His cross. And you, who once were alienated and enemies in your mind by wicked works, yet now He has reconciled in the body of His flesh through death, to present you holy, and blameless, and irreproachable in His sight ...."*

Heb. 2:17 *"Therefore, in all things He had to be made like His brethren, that He might be a merciful and faithful High Priest in things pertaining to God, to make propitiation for the sins of the people."*

● *The death of Christ actually justifies* the believer because His shed blood was the propitiation for sin and was acceptable to God. Redemption is the actual setting free from the bondage of sin by the blood of Christ to serve the living God.

Rom. 3:24-25 *"... being justified freely by His grace through the redemption that is in Christ Jesus, whom God set forth to be a propitiation by His blood, through faith, to demonstrate His righteousness, because in His forbearance God had passed over the sins that were previously committed."*

Rom. 5:8- 9 *"But God demonstrates His own love toward us, in that while we were still sinners, Christ died for us. Much more then, having now been justified by His blood, we shall be saved from wrath through Him."*

Rom. 5:18 *"Therefore, as through one man's offense judgment came to all men, resulting in condemnation, even so through one Man's righteous act the free gift came to all men, resulting in justification of life."*

I Cor. 1:30 *"But of Him you are in Christ Jesus, who became for us wisdom from God – and righteousness and sanctification and re-demption."*

Gal. 2:16 *"Knowing that a man is not justified by the works of the law but by faith in Jesus Christ, even we have believed in Christ Jesus, that we might be justified by faith in Christ and not by the works of the law; for by the works of the law no flesh shall be justified."*

Gal. 3:13 *"Christ has redeemed us from the curse of the law, having become a curse for us (for it is written, Cursed is everyone who hangs on a tree)."*

Gal. 4:4-5 *"But when the fullness of the time had come, God sent forth His Son, born of a woman, born under the law, to redeem those who were under the law, that we might receive the adoption as sons."*

Col. 1:13-14 *"He has delivered us from the power of darkness and translated us into the kingdom of the Son of His love, in whom we have redemption through His blood, the forgiveness of sins."*

Heb. 9:12 *"Not with the blood of goats and calves, but with His own blood He entered the Most Holy Place once for all, having obtained eternal redemption."*

Heb. 10:14 *"For by one offering He has perfected forever those who are being sanctified."*

I Pet. 1:18-19 *"Knowing that you were not redeemed with corruptible things, like silver or gold, from your aimless conduct received by tradition from your fathers, but with the precious blood of Christ, as of a lamb without blemish and without spot."*

I Pet. 2:24 *"Who Himself bore our sins in His own body on the tree, that we, having died to sins, might live for righteousness – by whose stripes you were healed."*

I Jn. 1:7 *"But if we walk in the light as He is in the light, we have fellowship with one another, and the blood of Jesus Christ His Son cleanses us from all sin."*

● Regeneration by the Holy Spirit is necessary for us to have true faith, and thereby to be saved. The gift of *the Holy Spirit to regenerate and sanctify is actually given* to all whom Christ died for.

John 3:3 *"Jesus answered and said to him, Most assuredly, I say to you, unless one is born again, he cannot see the kingdom of God."*

Acts 16:14 *"Now a certain woman named Lydia heard us. She was a seller of purple from the city of Thyatira, who worshiped God. The Lord opened her heart to heed the things spoken by Paul."*

Eph. 1:13, 14 *"In Him you also trusted, after you heard the word of truth, the gospel of your salvation; in whom also, having believed, you were sealed with the Holy Spirit of promise, who is the* *guarantee of our inheritance until the redemption of the purchased possession, to the praise of His glory."*

Titus 3:5, 6 *"Not by works of righteousness which we have done, but according to His mercy He saved us, through the washing of regeneration and renewing of the Holy Spirit, whom He poured out on us abundantly through Jesus Christ our Savior."*

I Cor. 1:30 *"But of Him you are in Christ Jesus, who became for us wisdom from God – and righteousness and sanctification and redemption."*

II Thess. 2:13 *"But we are bound to give thanks to God always for you, brethren beloved by the Lord, because God from the beginning chose you for salvation through sanctification by the Spirit and belief in the truth."*

Heb. 9:14 *"How much more shall the blood of Christ, who through the eternal Spirit offered Himself without spot to God, purge your conscience from dead works to serve the living God?"*

I Pet. 1:2 *"Elect according to the foreknowledge of God the Father, in sanctification of the Spirit, for obedience and sprinkling of the blood of Jesus Christ: Grace to you and peace be multiplied."*

2. There are a number of Bible passages that give us a glimpse of the purpose of Christ in fulfilling the covenant with His Father made before the foundation of the world. In summary, *Jesus laid down His life for those whom the Father had "given" to Him.* Read **John 6:35-40** and **John 17** carefully.

3. Jesus is conscious of laying down His life *for "His sheep."* Those who are not believers are not "His sheep" (Jn. 10:26).

John 10:24-29 *"Then the Jews surrounded Him and said to Him, How long do You keep us in doubt? If You are the Christ, tell us plainly. Jesus answered them, I told you, and you do not believe. The works that I do in My Father's name, they bear witness of Me. But you do not believe, because you are not of My sheep, as I said to you. My sheep hear My voice, and I know them, and they follow Me. And I give them eternal life, and they shall never perish; neither shall anyone snatch them out of My hand. My Father, who has given them to Me, is greater than all; and no one is able to snatch them out of My Father's hand."* (see also John 10:11,14-18 and Matthew 25:31-46)

3. In the High Priestly prayer of Christ, Jesus does not pray for the world in general, but **for those who were given to him by his Father.**

> **John 17:2, 6, 9, 11, 12, 24** *"As You have given Him authority over all flesh, that He should give eternal life to as many as You have given Him. I have manifested Your name to the men whom You have given Me out of the world. They were Yours, You gave them to Me, and they have kept Your word. I pray for them. I do not pray for the world but for those whom You have given Me, for they are Yours. Now I am no longer in the world, but these are in the world, and I come to You. Holy Father, keep through Your name those whom You have given Me, that they may be one as We are. While I was with them in the world, I kept them in Your name. Those whom You gave Me I have kept; and none of them is lost except the son of perdition, that the Scripture might be fulfilled. Father, I desire that they also whom You gave Me may be with Me where I am, that they may behold My glory which You have given Me; for You loved Me before the foundation of the world."*

4. Christ "justified" those for whom He died (Rom. 5:9). If Christ bore the sins of all men without exception, then all men are justified. If all men are justified, then they receive Christ by faith and are at peace with God (Rom. 5:1). All who are justified are likewise glorified (Rom. 8:30). It is clear from the Bible as well as from the world in which we live that many live and die at enmity with God and are lost eternally. If Christ died for all, then all would be justified, and none would be lost. We see from the Bible and our world that this is not true.

QUESTIONS:

1. From the verses above list 5 passages in the order that will most clearly present this doctrine of Limited Atonement to a person who has never heard of it before.

2. Explain the context and meaning of three of the "universalist" passages in Chapter 11 and demonstrate how they do not contradict the doctrine of Limited Atonement.

3. Why is the term "sheep" an important one in understanding this

doctrine?

Match the following (there is one extra verse):

1___	The price of redemption	A. Eph. 1:13,14
2___	The Holy Spirit seals salvation.	B. Rom. 5:9
3___	Jesus died for His sheep.	C. Heb. 9:15
4___	Jesus' death actually saved.	D. I Pet. 1:18,19
5___	Jesus is the Mediator of the	E. John 17:2
	New Testament.	F. John 10:11
6___	Jesus died for those given to Him.	G. II Cor. 5:18
7___	Reconciled by Christ	H. I Tim. 1:15
8___	Justified by Christ's blood	I. Matt. 22:46

13

The Doctrine of
Irresistible Grace
Part 1

A Trinitarian Work

Each member of the Trinity – the Father, the Son, and the Holy Spirit – participates in and is vital to the salvation of all sinners. In order to see the place of the doctrine of *irresistible grace* in the plan of God's salvation of man, it is necessary to briefly review what we have established as the teaching of Scripture thus far.

As we have already seen, it is necessary for God to sovereignly come to man to save him, because man in his natural state of *total depravity* will not and can not come to Christ by himself. Rather, he is prone to hate God and his neighbor (*Heidelberg Catechism* Q. 5), and therefore will not and cannot love God or serve Him.

The *Father*, before the foundation of the world, choose or elected those whom He predestined to save. This *election was unconditional*. The ground of God's choice was His sovereign will and love, not any merit foreseen in man. God gave His elected people to His Son, Jesus Christ, in order that Christ could make full atonement for their sin.

This *atonement was limited* in its purpose – to save the elect given to Jesus by His Father. *Jesus* fully paid for the sins of His people on the cross. But the work of the Father and the Son do not complete the work of salvation, because the work of Jesus still needs to be applied to the hearts of God's elect, because man's will is in bondage to sin (of which unbelief and rebellion are a part). If man is going to "receive" the benefits of Christ, he must have a heart to receive it.

God does not provide a cafeteria-style salvation where it is all prepared, attractively laid out, and left to man to take or leave. Rather, God comes to His elect for whom Christ shed His blood and *applies to them salvation through the power of His Word and Holy Spirit.* It is this grace of God in applying salvation that is the subject of the doctrine of *irresistible grace.* The person of the Trinity that is primarily active in this work of God is His Holy Spirit.

Simply stated, this doctrine declares that *the Holy Spirit never fails to bring to salvation those sinners whom He personally and sovereignly calls to repentance and faith in Christ.* All those that God intends to save – and indeed has saved in Christ – will be saved. This is because the Holy Spirit will apply the truth of the gospel to the heart of the elect whom He has regenerated. He does this *sovereignly, irresistibly, and unfailingly.* Man has neither the power nor the desire (after regeneration) to *resist the call* of the gospel. To maintain, as Arminians do, that man has the power to resist the almighty power of God is blasphemous and a great error.

The Holy Spirit of God, no less than the Father and the Son is sovereign. In John 3:8, the free and sovereign nature of the Spirit of God is described as follows: *"The wind blows where it wishes, and you hear the sound of it, but cannot tell where it comes from and where it goes. So is everyone who is born of the Spirit.* It should be remembered that the word for "wind", "breath", and "Spirit" are from the same Greek word (*"pneuma"*). The word *"wind"* here refers to the Holy Spirit.

Earlier we mentioned that Christ's atonement was limited, not because it was "insufficient" to save all men, but that it was "efficient", "effectual", and intended only for the elect. This "effectual" characteristic of the atonement is dependant upon the Holy Spirit actually applying Christ's cleansing blood to His people. The *certainty* that God's Holy Spirit will apply the benefits of salvation, are based on the fact that God has *certainly chosen* His people unto salvation and Christ has *certainly died* for them. In summary, those who were dead in sin, elected by God's grace, and redeemed by Christ's blood *will believe.*

The External Call of the Gospel

The gospel call or command (that is, to repent of sin and believe in Jesus) extends to all who hear the sound of the gospel. It summons all men to come to Christ by way of repentance and faith to receive His righteousness and everlasting life, or if they refuse to believe, to suffer the wrath of God and everlasting condemnation.

Given the fact that we do not know who the elect are when we bring the gospel to them, we bring it with sincerity to all men. We call all men to repent and believe the gospel with the full realization that God will only apply it to His elect. Man, left to himself, cannot believe it. The *Canons of Dort* also teach this in the Third and Fourth Heads of Doctrine, Article 8: *"As many as are called by the gospel are unfeignedly (sincerely) called. For God has most earnestly and truly declared in His Word what is acceptable to Him, namely that those who are called should come unto Him. He also seriously promises rest of soul and eternal life to all who come to Him and believe."*

This *external or outward call of the gospel* alone will not bring anyone to salvation. Why? Because man, by nature is dead in sin and under its power! The carnal, fallen nature will not and cannot respond in faith to the gospel. No amount of light can penetrate his blind eyes. No amount of logic or persuasion can convince an understanding that is darkened by sin. No amount of truth will pierce his deaf ears. No power of man can raise up to life the sinner's dead heart. *"Because the carnal mind is enmity against God; for it is not subject to the law of God, nor indeed can be. So then, those who are in the flesh cannot please God."* (Romans 8:7, 8) Again Jesus says in John 6:44, *"No one can come to Me unless the Father who sent Me draws him; and I will raise him up at the last day."*

The *Canons of Dort,* Third and Fourth Heads of Doctrine,

Article 9 says: *"It is not the fault of the gospel, nor of Christ offered therein, nor of God, who calls men by the gospel and confers upon them various gifts, that those who are called by the ministry of the Word refuse to come and be converted. The fault lies in themselves...."*

Before man can believe the message of salvation, the Holy Spirit of God must change the sinner's heart of stone into a heart of flesh – it must be reborn or resurrected from death to life. Since man does not have a free will by nature (but one in bondage to sin and Satan since the Fall), the Holy Spirit must first change (set free) the will of man so that it conforms to the will of God. In speaking of Lydia's conversion we read, *"The Lord opened her heart to heed the things spoken by Paul."* (Acts 16:14b) *"For it is God who works in you both to will and to do for His good pleasure."* (Phil. 2:13)

The Inward Call of the Holy Spirit

In order for the Holy Spirit to bring God's elect people to a saving faith, He applies, along with the external call of the gospel, His special *inward call*. He does this by *regenerating* (bringing back to life) the dead heart. He then gives us an understanding of the gospel so that we see our sin and misery and trust in the sacrifice of Christ as the only ground of our salvation.

The Canons of Dort, Third and Fourth Heads of Doctrine, Article 11 says, *"But when God accomplishes His good pleasure in the elect, or works in them true conversion, He not only causes the gospel to be externally preached to them, and powerfully illuminates their minds by His Holy Spirit, that they may rightly understand and discern the things of the Spirit of God; but by the efficacy of the same regenerating Spirit He pervades the inmost recesses of man; He opens the closed and softens the hardened heart, and circumcises that which was uncircumcised; infuses new qualities into the will, which, though heretofore dead, He quickens; from being evil, disobedient, and refractory, He renders it good, obedient, and pliable; actuates and strengthens it, that like a good tree, it may bring forth the fruits of good actions."*

The Holy Spirit works faith in our hearts once He has prepared the heart. Much like the Parable of the Sower of Matthew 13, the Holy Spirit is the one who makes the "field" fertile so it can receive the seed of the gospel, cause it take root, grow, and bear fruits of faith.

The Holy Spirit does not work "with" the Word in the sense that every time the Word of God is proclaimed the Holy Spirit is attempting to apply it to all who hear it but is unsuccessful insofar as some reject His work. Rather, it is more correct to say that the Holy Spirit *works "through" the Word* to teach and apply its truths to those whom God has chosen. The Holy Spirit works sovereignly in the application of the gospel.

The Effects of the Word and the Holy Spirit

Could we say that the gospel message has failed if many who hear it do not believe? Is it without any effect at all in the ears of the reprobate? Not at all. As one of the *Keys to the Kingdom* of God, the preaching of the gospel *opens* the door to the kingdom of heaven to all who in true faith receive the gospel, and it *closes* the doors to all who do not repent and believe (see *Heidelberg Catechism* Q. 84).

The preaching of the gospel has the *effect either of saving or condemning*. It is never without God's decreed results. The preaching of the gospel *never fails in its purpose*. *"So shall My word be that goes forth from My mouth; it shall not return to Me void, but it shall accomplish what I please, and it shall prosper in the thing for which I sent it."* (Is. 55:11) Not only does the Word of God never fail, but the Holy Spirit never fails to apply it to God's people.

A Freed Will Instead of a Free Will

When we say that the work of the Holy Spirit in applying the saving work of Christ is *"irresistible,"* we should not misunderstand this concept. To some people it may appear as though man was caused to do something that he did not want to do. God does not drag His elect people into heaven against their wills, struggling and kicking against Him. By the regeneration of the heart man is *made willing* to believe the gospel. His will is renewed through the power of the Spirit so that in due time he humbly believes by his own freed will – a will set free that it may submit to the Word of God.

Man does not come to faith in some mechanical fashion so that he does not actually realize what he is doing. The *Canons of Dort*, Third and Fourth Head of Doctrine, Article 16 says, *"this grace of regeneration does not treat men as senseless stocks and blocks, nor take away their will and its properties, or do violence thereto...."* What the Holy Spirit does is to *change man's will* (sets it free) so that he is now both willing and able to repent of his sin and believe in Jesus for salvation. He now has a *freed* will.

God does not just create in man the ability to believe and then leave it to man's free will to accomplish the terms of salvation. *"Faith is therefore to be considered as the gift of God, not on account of its being offered by God to man, to be accepted or rejected as his pleasure, but because it is in reality conferred upon him, breathed and infused into him; nor even because God bestows the power or ability to believe, and then expects that man should by the exercise of his own free will consent to the terms of salvation and actually believe in Christ, but because He who works in man both will and to work, and indeed all things in all, produces both the will to believe and the act of believing also."* (*Canons of Dort* Chapters III & 4, Article 14; see Phil. 2:13).

God saves in a way that the regenerate man enjoys. Man never goes to heaven against his will. The regenerated will desires nothing more than to have everlasting life and communion with His gracious and loving God and Father. On the contrary, the unbeliever who has never repented and believed in Christ, but has laughed at all the warnings about eternal punishment and continued to live in the darkness of sin, gets exactly what he wants – everlasting separation from the grace of God.

By the sovereign and irresistible grace of the Holy Spirit the hearts of God's elect are changed so that they will earnestly hate sin and repent of sin and at the same time love God and believe in His Son as their Savior (see *Heidelberg Catechism* Q's 88-90). The Bible tells us that before man can love God, God must first love him. I Jn. 4:10 and 19 teach us, *"In this is love, not that we loved God, but that He loved us and sent His Son to be the propitiation for our sins. We love Him because He first loved us."* To have faith, man does have to know the Word of God (*"How shall they call on Him in whim they have not believed? And how shall they believe in Him of whom they have not heard? And how shall they hear without a preacher? So then faith comes by hearing, and hearing by the word of God."* (Rom. 10:14, 17) Man does not respond to the love of God by *just* hearing or reading about it. Man only knows of God's love with true faith *after* God sends His Spirit to bring the heart back to life.

Since the hand of God is almighty, there is no power in man or in Satan to resist or to hinder the grace of God to save His people. This is one of the greatest comforts a Christian can have. In Question 1 of the *Heidelberg Catechism* we read of this comfort in this way, *"...wherefore by his Holy Spirit He also assures me of eternal life, and makes me heartily willing and ready from now on to live unto Him."*

Questions:

1. Explain the difference between the external and internal call of the gospel.

2. What do the Canons of Dort refer to when they say that man is not a "senseless stock or block"?

3. If the unregenerate person refuses to heed the call of the gospel, does this destroy the doctrine of "irresistible grace"?   Explain.

4. What does the Holy Spirit do to the will of man in regeneration?

   • Why is this not a mechanical way to save man?

   • Explain why we still present the gospel "sincerely" to all men.

5. What is the difference between a "free" will and a "freed" will?

6. Describe the work of each person of the Trinity in saving us, as we have studied it thus far.

7. In what sense can we say that in the end, everyone gets what they wanted?

14

The Doctrine of Irresistible Grace Part 2

A Perilous Position

The position that says "God wants to save all men; He sent Christ to die for all men; and He sends His Holy Spirit to call men, but He can't save man because man is able to resist the Holy Spirit" is a dangerous one and dishonoring to our sovereign God. The doctrines of Arminianism teach that man does need the Holy Spirit's *help* in to be saved. This help comes *after* faith. But, this help may be *resisted* by man, so that he does not believe.

When asked the question of "Who did Christ die for?", the answer often given is "For all believers." While that may sound correct, it betrays a lack of understanding and possibly the misunderstanding of Arminianism which says that Christ died for those who were elected by the "foresight" of God (based on God being able to foresee who would believe and then electing them). It is more accurate, if we want to use this type of language to say that "Christ died in order that His people might believe and be saved." It must be the Spirit that brings the elect people of God to believe or they never would.

When the Bible speaks about quenching the Spirit (*"Do not quench the Spirit."* - I Thess. 5:19), this is not in reference to the act of regeneration or conversion, but the actions of believing Christians who sin against God. It is the quenching of the sanctifying work of the Holy Spirit (not the regenerating work) that this refers to. The old nature of Adam that still clings to Christians causes them to quench the work of the Spirit in their lives. This is a sin and must be repented of. Certainly all unbelievers do resist the Truth of God – this is the very essence of their depravity. *"Now as Jannes and Jambres resisted Moses, so do these also resist the truth: men of corrupt minds, disapproved concerning the faith."* (II Tim. 3:8) However, neither of these passages teach that these men resisted the attempt of the Holy Spirit to regenerate their hearts.

At best, according to Arminianism, God can only expect some sort of cooperation between His grace and man's choice. The result of this is to view man and God on an equal basis. We are on very false and dangerous ground anytime the Creator and the creature are seen as equals. Even worse, if the creature can halt the will of the Creator by his stubbornness, *then man is god and is his own idol.*

It is said by some that *God will never coerce or never force you to do His will.* This is also a false and dangerous statement. As we have seen, the method that God employs to carry out his will is to change the will of man that it surrenders to His. While He does not force His will on man in a human sense, He does cause the mind of man to accept His will. In the conversion of the Apostle Paul, it certainly does appear obvious that God overpowered him. Certainly, there is no indication in Paul that he was "softening up" to the message of the gospel prior to Christ confronting him on the road to Damascus.

It is dangerous to say that God can do no more than present you an *offer.* This makes Him no more than a salesman trying to convince mankind to buy His product. We see this attitude displayed in the methodologies employed by some to market the gospel in today's churches.

Arminianism says, 'There is one area of your life that God will never touch – your will. He will never cause you to believe. That's your job. Only you can do it.' This is simply contrary to the Bible. Lydia knew the efficacious grace of God: *"Now a certain woman named Lydia heard us. She was a seller of purple from the city of Thyatira, who worshiped God. The Lord opened her heart to heed the things spoken by Paul.*" (Acts 16:14) Jesus express this in John 6:65, "*And He said, Therefore I have said to you that no one can come to Me unless it has been granted to him by My Father.*"

Regeneration

It is very important to see *what regeneration is and that it precedes faith.* Regeneration is the sovereign act of God by His Holy Spirit whereby he *implants new life* (a new heart) into man so that *the thoughts and inclinations of man's heart are disposed unto holiness.* God creates a hunger and thirst for the bread and living water which comes from heaven. The Bible calls regeneration being "born again" or "born of the Spirit"). John 3 relates the conversation of Nicodemus and Jesus: "*This man came to Jesus by night and said to Him, Rabbi, we know that You are a teacher come from God; for no one can do these signs that You do unless God is with him. Jesus answered and said to him, Most assuredly, I say to you, unless one is born again, he cannot see the kingdom of God.*" In order to explain to Nicodemus that this new birth is from above, He said, "*That which is born of the flesh is flesh, and that which is born of the Spirit is spirit. Do not marvel that I said to you, You must be born again. The wind blows where it wishes, and you hear the sound of it, but cannot tell where it comes from and where it goes. So is everyone who is born of the Spirit.*" (Jn. 3:2-3, 6-8)

Without doubt regeneration is necessary for a Christian to understand the Scriptures, to be convicted of sin, to repent, and to believe. This is the miracle which God performs in us. "*Jesus answered and said to him, "Most assuredly, I say to you, unless one is born again, he cannot see the kingdom of God. Jesus answered, Most assuredly, I say to you, unless one is born of water and the Spirit, he cannot enter the kingdom of God.*" (Jn. 3:3, 5) It is impossible to see or to enter the kingdom of God apart from this rebirth.

Likewise Paul says in I Cor. 2:14 "*But the natural man does not receive the things of the Spirit of God, for they are foolishness to him; nor can he know them, because they are spiritually discerned.*" The "*natural man*" is the unregenerate man fallen in Adam. Man *cannot* know or discern the gospel message spoken to Him unless he has the Spirit of God. Notice what I Cor. 2:12 tells us, *"Now we have received, not the spirit of the world, but the Spirit who is from God, that we might know the things that have been freely given to us by God."*

Question 8 of the *Heidelberg Catechism* teaches, "Are we so depraved that we are completely incapable of any good and prone to all evil? Yes, unless we are born again by the Spirit of God." And again in Question 21 in defining "true faith," the catechism says that "true faith is not only a sure knowledge, whereby I hold for truth all that God has revealed to us in His Word, but also a hearty trust, *which the Holy Ghost works in me* by the gospel...." It is the knowledge, the holding for truth, and the heartfelt trust that are the results of the Holy Spirit's work in us.

While regeneration is the beginning of the Christian's new life, it does not end there. It inevitably results in *conversion* – in true repentance and faith. After that, the Holy Spirit continues to *sanctify* His people – to cause them to live lives of godliness, holiness, and thankfulness as Paul says in II Cor. 5:17,18, *"Therefore, if anyone is in Christ, he is a new creation; old things have passed away; behold, all things have become new. Now all things are of God, who has reconciled us to Himself through Jesus Christ, and has given us the ministry of reconciliation."*

Paul's conversion on the road to Damascus is quite unique in its suddenness and miraculous fashion. Immediately after our Lord came to him, the work of the Holy Spirit was clearly displayed by his words, *"Lord, what do you want me to do?"* (Acts 9:6) Paul did not resist, even though, of all men, we might think that he would have fought fiercely against it. What God does as He plants faith in the hearts of His people is to take away the sinful will to resist.

While each Christian's conversion may not be that dramatic, Paul's conversion is to be seen as a *pattern* of what takes place in the life of the unbeliever as he becomes a Christian. Notice what Paul says in I Timothy 1:15-16, *"This is a faithful saying and worthy of all acceptance, that Christ Jesus came into the world to save sinners, of whom I am chief. However, for this reason I obtained mercy, that in me first Jesus Christ might show all longsuffering, as a pattern to those who are going to believe on Him for everlasting life."*

God's grace is *always efficacious.* It always accomplishes the purposes of God, and cannot be cast aside by man. As Isaiah says, *"For My thoughts are not your thoughts, nor are your ways My ways, says the LORD. For as the heavens are higher than the earth, so are My ways higher than your ways, and My thoughts than your thoughts. For as the rain comes down, and the snow from heaven, and do not return there, but water the earth, and make it bring forth and bud, that it may give seed to the sower and bread to the eater, so shall My word be that goes forth from My mouth; it shall not return to Me void, but it shall accomplish what I please, and it shall prosper in the thing for which I sent it."* (Is. 55:8-11)

How the Spirit Works in Us

"How then shall they call on him in whom they have not believed? and how shall they believe in him of whom they have not heard? and how shall they hear without a preacher? And how shall they preach, except they be sent? as it is written, How beautiful are the feet of them that preach the gospel of peace, and bring glad tidings of good things! But they have not all obeyed the gospel. For Esaias saith, Lord, who hath believed our report? So then faith cometh by hearing, and hearing by the word of God." (Rom. 10:14-17)

It is by the *preaching and teaching of the gospel* that God, through His Holy Spirit, works faith in His people. *"For Christ did not send me to baptize, but to preach the gospel, not with wisdom of words, lest the cross of Christ should be made of no effect. For the message of the cross is foolishness to those who are perishing, but to us who are being saved it is the power of God. For since, in the wisdom of God, the world through wisdom did not know God, it pleased God through the foolishness of the message preached to save those who believe. But we preach Christ crucified, to the Jews a stumbling block and to the Greeks foolishness."* (I Cor. 1:17, 18, 21, 23; cf. Rom. 10:14-18)

The words that Jesus left as a commission to the Church said, *"Go therefore and make disciples of all the nations, baptizing them in*

*the name of the Father and of the Son and of the Holy Spirit, teaching
them to observe all things that I have commanded you; and lo, I am
with you always, even to the end of the age. Amen."* (Matt. 28:19-20)

As we have seen in the previous chapter, we cannot say that
the Holy Spirit works "with" the Word, but, rather, that He works
"through" the Word. If He works "with" the Word, then whenever the
Word is preached, the Holy Spirit would be applying, or attempting to
apply, saving grace to all who heard. All who did not believe could be
said to have "resisted" the Holy Spirit. It is more scriptural to say that
the Holy Spirit works "through" the Word to work faith in the hearts
of God's elect. That is, God has chosen this "method" to save His
people.

Since faith results from the hearing of the Word of God
preached, the Christian Church does not (and should not) rely on the
"packaging", but on the "power of God". Romans 1:16 tells us, *"For
I am not ashamed of the gospel of Christ, for it is the power of God to
salvation for everyone who believes, for the Jew first and also for the
Greek."* Again, Paul tells the Corinthians in I Cor. 1:18, *"For the
message of the cross is foolishness to those who are perishing, but to
us who are being saved it is the power of God."*

Arminianism must rely heavily on the power of the *messenger*
rather than the power of the Word, since it is largely left in his hands
to cause the hearers to believe. This has become the mark of many
churches today – to package the gospel attractively with entertainment
or personalities. The congregation is then built around a person or a
movement. This is a grave error, which some do not try hard enough
to discourage, and some actually encourage.

Such methods of evangelism are foreign to the Bible. As a
matter of fact the greatest of all missionaries of the church, Paul, says
in I Cor. 2:4,5 *"And my speech and my preaching were not with
persuasive words of human wisdom, but in demonstration of the Spirit
and of power, that your faith should not be in the wisdom of men but
in the power of God."* Again, Paul says, *"But God has revealed them
to us through His Spirit. For the Spirit searches all things, yes, the
deep things of God. For what man knows the things of a man except
the spirit of the man which is in him? Even so no one knows the things*

of God except the Spirit of God. Now we have received, not the spirit of the world, but the Spirit who is from God, that we might know the things that have been freely given to us by God. These things we also speak, not in words which man's wisdom teaches but which the Holy Spirit teaches, comparing spiritual things with spiritual." (I Cor. 2:10-13) Paul's obvious desire is to have all attention drawn away from himself and directed to the power of the Holy Spirit. *"Who then is Paul, and who is Apollos, but ministers through whom you believed, as the Lord gave to each one? I planted, Apollos watered, but God gave the increase."* and *"Therefore let no one boast in men...."* (I Cor. 3:5, 6, 21)

It is a great sin if the Church abandons preaching as something ineffective or outdated and adopts the methods of the world in order to have a greater appeal with the gospel. It is common for people to think nothing of the "method," as long as it appears to work. The question of how the church should engage in its duties ought never to be answered by "Does it work?," but "Is it faithful to the revealed will of God?"

Does anything man-centered really work? If the basis of man's faith is not the truth, then it is not a faith that will last, and indeed, it is not a faith that works. True faith cannot come from a false gospel. *"For no other foundation can anyone lay than that which is laid, which is Jesus Christ. Now if anyone builds on this foundation with gold, silver, precious stones, wood, hay, straw, each one's work will become manifest; for the Day will declare it, because it will be revealed by fire; and the fire will test each one's work, of what sort it is."* (I Cor. 3:11-13) When we become "growth" oriented or "success" oriented in bringing the gospel to the world, we stand in grave danger of conforming the Word to the world instead of seeking to conform the world to the Word. The Holy Spirit works faith with the true gospel, not a false gospel (cf. Gal. 1:6-12).

God's Word is powerful and has a powerful impact on those whom God has given a heart transplant. Hebrews 4:12 and 13 tells us, *"For the word of God is living and powerful, and sharper than any two-edged sword, piercing even to the division of soul and spirit, and of joints and marrow, and is a discerner of the thoughts and intents of the heart.   And there is no creature hidden from His sight, but all things are naked and open to the eyes of Him to whom we must give account."*

It is then, through the power of the Word of God that God's Holy Spirit works faith in the hearts of the elect who have been regenerated by the Spirit of God. The power of the Word and the power of the Holy Spirit are infinitely greater than the power of man to resist.

Questions:

1. What are the dangers present in the doctrine of the Arminians who hold that God's Spirit can be resisted?

2. What is wrong with this expression concerning Christianity, *"I found it!"*?

3. In what sense can we say that men do "resist" the gospel?

4. Given the Arminian doctrine about how man believes, why are various and ever-changing "methods" necessary?

   • Give examples of false methods:
   • What method has God provided to build His church?
5. What is meant by "regeneration"?

   • Which comes first, faith or regeneration? and Why?

6. Acts 2:47 says, "And the Lord added to the church daily such those who were being saved." What connection does this have with the doctrine of irresistible grace?

7. Explain the connection of irresistible grace with total depravity, unconditional election, and limited atonement.

8. In what way is the conversion of Paul a help in understanding the irresistible nature of God's grace?

9. How does the Apostle Paul describe the power of his preaching in I Cor. 2?

   • How did Paul feel about those who said, "We go to Paul's church," according to I Cor. 3?

15

The Doctrine of
Irresistible Grace
Part 3

The Bible gives ample evidence that the Holy Spirit of God must sovereignly apply the work of salvation to the individual, and that it is the Holy Spirit who empowers the church to preach the gospel of Christ for the gathering and building of the church. The reason that there is much evidence of this work is because it is so closely tied with the doctrine of total depravity. If man is unwilling and unable, by his own free will, to believe the gospel, then God must work faith in the hearts of His elect people by the power of His Spirit.

Outline and Proofs from the Bible

1. Salvation is Trinitarian in its scope -- involving the *Holy Spirit* as well as the Father and the Son.

> **Rom. 8:14** *"For as many as are led by the Spirit of God, these are sons of God."*

> **I Cor. 2:10-14** *"But God has revealed them to us through His Spirit. For the Spirit searches all things, yes, the deep things of God. For what man knows the things of a man except the spirit of the man*

which is in him? Even so no one knows the things of God except the Spirit of God. Now we have received, not the spirit of the world, but the Spirit who is from God, that we might know the things that have been freely given to us by God. These things we also speak, not in words which man's wisdom teaches but which the Holy Spirit teaches, comparing spiritual things with spiritual. But the natural man does not receive the things of the Spirit of God, for they are foolishness to him; nor can he know them, because they are spiritually discerned."

1 Cor. 6:11 *"And such were some of you. But you were washed, but you were sanctified, but you were justified in the name of the Lord Jesus and by the Spirit of our God."*

1 Cor. 12:3 *"Therefore I make known to you that no one speaking by the Spirit of God calls Jesus accursed, and no one can say that Jesus is Lord except by the Holy Spirit."*

II Cor. 3:6 *"... who also made us sufficient as ministers of the new covenant, not of the letter but of the Spirit; for the letter kills, but the Spirit gives life."*

II Cor. 3:17 *"Now the Lord is the Spirit; and where the Spirit of the Lord is, there is liberty."*

II Cor. 3:18 *"But we all, with unveiled face, beholding as in a mirror the glory of the Lord, are being transformed into the same image from glory to glory, just as by the Spirit of the Lord."*

I Pet. 1:2 *"... elect according to the foreknowledge of God the Father, in sanctification of the Spirit, for obedience and sprinkling of the blood of Jesus Christ: Grace to you and peace be multiplied."*

2. Sinners, through regeneration, are brought into God's kingdom and made His children. The *author of this new birth is the Holy Spirit*. The *instrument* which He uses is the preaching of the Word of God.

John 1:12-13 *"But as many as received Him, to them He gave the right to become children of God, even to those who believe in His name: who were born, not of blood, nor of the will of the flesh, nor of the will of man, but of God."*

John 3:3-8 *"Jesus answered and said to him, Most assuredly, I say to you, unless one is born again, he cannot see the kingdom of God. Nicodemus said to Him, How can a man be born when he is old? Can he enter a second time into his mother's womb and be born?*

Jesus answered, Most assuredly, I say to you, unless one is born of water and the Spirit, he cannot enter the kingdom of God. That which is born of the flesh is flesh, and that which is born of the Spirit is spirit. Do not marvel that I said to you, You must be born again. The wind blows where it wishes, and you hear the sound of it, but cannot tell where it comes from and where it goes. So is everyone who is born of the Spirit."

Titus 3:5-7 *"... not by works of righteousness which we have done, but according to His mercy He saved us, through the washing of regeneration and renewing of the Holy Spirit, whom He poured out on us abundantly through Jesus Christ our Savior, that having been justified by His grace we should become heirs according to the hope of eternal life."*

I Pet. 1:3, 23-25 *"Blessed be the God and Father of our Lord Jesus Christ, who according to His abundant mercy has begotten us again to a living hope through the resurrection of Jesus Christ from the dead... having been born again, not of corruptible seed but incorruptible, through the word of God which lives and abides forever, because All flesh is as grass, and all the glory of man as the flower of the grass. The grass withers, and its flower falls away, but the word of the Lord endures forever. Now this is the word which by the gospel was preached to you."*

I John 5:4 *"For whatever is born of God overcomes the world. And this is the victory that has overcome the world – our faith."*

3. Through the work of the Holy Spirit man is given a *new heart* (nature) and made to walk according to the will of God. Man becomes a *new creature* in Jesus Christ.

> **Deut. 30:6** *"And the LORD your God will circumcise your heart and the heart of your descendants, to love the LORD your God with all your heart and with all your soul, that you may live."*

> **Jer. 31:33-34** *"But this is the covenant that I will make with the house of Israel: After those days, says the LORD, I will put My law in their minds, and write it on their hearts; and I will be their God, and they shall be My people. No more shall every man teach his neighbor, and every man his brother, saying, Know the LORD, for they all shall know Me, from the least of them to the greatest of them, says the LORD. For I will forgive their iniquity, and their sin I will remember no more."*

Ezek. 36:26-27 *"I will give you a new heart and put a new spirit within you; I will take the heart of stone out of your flesh and give you a heart of flesh. I will put My Spirit within you and cause you to walk in My statutes, and you will keep My judgments and do them."*

Gal. 6:15 *"For in Christ Jesus neither circumcision nor uncircumcision avails anything, but a new creation."*

Eph. 2:10, 18, 22 *"For we are His workmanship, created in Christ Jesus for good works, which God prepared beforehand that we should walk in them. For through Him we both have access by one Spirit to the Father. ... in whom you also are being built together for a habitation of God in the Spirit."*

II Cor.5:17-18 *"Therefore, if anyone is in Christ, he is a new creation; old things have passed away; behold, all things have become new. Now all things are of God, who has reconciled us to Himself through Jesus Christ, and has given us the ministry of reconciliation."*

4. The Holy Spirit *raises man* from a state of *spiritual death to life.*

John 5:21 *"For as the Father raises the dead and gives life to them, even so the Son gives life to whom He will."*

Eph. 2:1, 5 *"And you He made alive, who were dead in trespasses and sins, ... even when we were dead in trespasses, made us alive together with Christ (by grace you have been saved)."*

Col. 2:13 *"And you, being dead in your trespasses and the uncircumcision of your flesh, He has made alive together with Him, having forgiven you all trespasses,"*

5. God *reveals to His elect the secrets of His kingdom* through the inward, personal revelation given by the Holy Spirit.

Matt. 11:25-27 *"At that time Jesus answered and said, I thank You, Father, Lord of heaven and earth, because You have hidden these things from the wise and prudent and have revealed them to babes. Even so, Father, for so it seemed good in Your sight. All things have been delivered to Me by My Father, and no one knows the Son except the Father. Nor does anyone know the Father except the Son, and he to whom the Son wills to reveal Him."*

Matt. 13:10-11, 16 *"And the disciples came and said to Him, Why do You speak to them in parables? He answered and said to them,*

Because it has been given to you to know the mysteries of the kingdom of heaven, but to them it has not been given. But blessed are your eyes for they see, and your ears for they hear."

Matt. 16:15-17 *"He said to them, But who do you say that I am? And Simon Peter answered and said, You are the Christ, the Son of the living God. Jesus answered and said to him, Blessed are you, Simon Bar-Jonah, for flesh and blood has not revealed this to you, but My Father who is in heaven."*

Luke 8:10 *"And He said, To you it has been given to know the mysteries of the kingdom of God, but to the rest it is given in parables, that Seeing they may not see, and hearing they may not understand."*

Luke 10:21 *"In that hour Jesus rejoiced in the Spirit and said, "I praise You, Father, Lord of heaven and earth, that You have hidden these things from the wise and prudent and revealed them to babes. Even so, Father, for so it seemed good in Your sight."*

John 6:37, 44-45, 64-65 *"All that the Father gives Me will come to Me, and the one who comes to Me I will by no means cast out. No one can come to Me unless the Father who sent Me draws him; and I will raise him up at the last day. It is written in the prophets, And they shall all be taught by God. Therefore everyone who has heard and learned from the Father comes to Me. But there are some of you who do not believe. For Jesus knew from the beginning who they were who did not believe, and who would betray Him. And He said, Therefore I have said to you that no one can come to Me unless it has been granted to him by My Father."*

John 10:3-6 *"To him the doorkeeper opens, and the sheep hear his voice; and he calls his own sheep by name and leads them out. And when he brings out his own sheep, he goes before them; and the sheep follow him, for they know his voice. Yet they will by no means follow a stranger, but will flee from him, for they do not know the voice of strangers. Jesus used this illustration, but they did not understand the things which He spoke to them."*

John 10:16 *"And other sheep I have which are not of this fold; them also I must bring, and they will hear My voice; and there will be one flock and one shepherd."*

John 10:26-29 *"But you do not believe, because you are not of My sheep, as I said to you. My sheep hear My voice, and I know them,* *and they follow Me. And I give them eternal life, and they shall never perish; neither shall anyone snatch them out of My hand. My Father, who has given them to Me, is greater than all; and no one is able to snatch them out of My Father's hand."*

I Cor. 2:11-14 *"For what man knows the things of a man except the spirit of the man which is in him? Even so no one knows the things of God except the Spirit of God. Now we have received, not the spirit of the world, but the Spirit who is from God, that we might know the things that have been freely given to us by God. These things we also speak, not in words which man's wisdom teaches but which the Holy Spirit teaches, comparing spiritual things with spiritual. But the natural man does not receive the things of the Spirit of God, for they are foolishness to him; nor can he know them, because they are spiritually discerned."*

Eph. 1:17-18 *"... that the God of our Lord Jesus Christ, the Father of glory, may give to you the spirit of wisdom and revelation in the know-ledge of Him, the eyes of your understanding being enlight-ened; that you may know what is the hope of His calling, what are the riches of the glory of His inheritance in the saints."*

6. *Faith and repentance are divine gifts* and are worked in the heart of the elect people of God through the regenerating work of the Holy Spirit.

Acts 5:31 *"Him God has exalted to His right hand to be Prince and Savior, to give repentance to Israel and forgiveness of sins."*

Acts 11:18 *"When they heard these things they became silent; and they glorified God, saying, Then God has also granted to the Gentiles repentance to life."*

Acts 13:48 *"Now when the Gentiles heard this, they were glad and glorified the word of the Lord. And as many as had been appointed to eternal life believed."*

Acts 16:14 *"Now a certain woman named Lydia heard us. She was a seller of purple from the city of Thyatira, who worshiped God. The Lord opened her heart to heed the things spoken by Paul."*

Acts 18:27 *"And when he desired to cross to Achaia, the brethren wrote, exhorting the disciples to receive him; and when he arrived, he greatly helped those who had believed through grace."*

Eph. 2:8-9 *"For by grace you have been saved through faith, and* *that not of yourselves; it is the gift of God, not of works, lest anyone should boast."*

Phil. 1:29 *"For to you it has been granted on behalf of Christ, not only to believe in Him, but also to suffer for His sake."*

II Tim. 2:25 *"... in humility correcting those who are in opposition, if God perhaps will grant them repentance, so that they may know the truth, and that they may come to their senses and escape the snare of the devil, having been taken captive by him to do his will."*

7. When the gospel is preached, there is a *general* (outward) *call* to salvation to all who hear its message. In addition to this general call, the Holy Spirit extends a *special, efficacious, call* to the elect only. The general call of the gospel can be, and often is rejected, but when this is *combined with the effectual inward call of the Holy Spirit, it cannot be resisted*; it always results in the conversion of those to whom it is made. These texts refer to this act of the Holy Spirit.

Rom. 1:6-7 *"among whom you also are the called of Jesus Christ; To all who are in Rome, beloved of God, called to be saints: Grace to you and peace from God our Father and the Lord Jesus Christ."*

Rom. 8:30 *"Moreover whom He predestined, these He also called; whom He called, these He also justified; and whom He justified, these He also glorified."*

Rom. 9:23-24 *"... and that He might make known the riches of His glory on the vessels of mercy, which He had prepared beforehand for glory, even us whom He called, not of the Jews only, but also of the Gentiles?"*

I Cor. 1:1-2, 9, 23-31 *"Paul, called to be an apostle of Jesus Christ through the will of God, and Sosthenes our brother, to the church of God which is at Corinth, to those who are sanctified in Christ Jesus, called to be saints, with all who in every place call on the name of Jesus Christ our Lord, both theirs and ours: God is faithful, by whom you were called into the fellowship of His Son, Jesus Christ our Lord. but we preach Christ crucified, to the Jews a stumbling block and to the Greeks foolishness, but to those who are called, both Jews and Greeks, Christ the power of God and the wisdom of God. Because the foolishness of God is wiser than men, and the weakness of God is stronger than men. For you see your calling, brethren, that not many wise according to the flesh, not many mighty, not many noble, are called. But God has chosen the foolish* *things of the world to put to shame the wise, and God has chosen the weak things of the world to put to shame the things which are mighty; and the base things of the world and the things which are despised God has chosen, and the things which are not, to bring to nothing the things that are, that no flesh should glory in His presence. But of Him you are in Christ Jesus, who became for us wisdom from God – and righteousness and sanctification and redemption – that, as it is written, He who glories, let him glory in the Lord."*

1 Cor. 2:4 *"And my speech and my preaching were not with persuasive words of human wisdom, but in demonstration of the Spirit and of power."*

Gal. 1:15-16 *"But when it pleased God, who separated me from my mother's womb and called me through His grace, to reveal His Son in me, that I might preach Him among the Gentiles, I did not immediately confer with flesh and blood."*

Eph. 4:4 *"There is one body and one Spirit, just as you were called in one hope of your calling."*

II Tim. 1:9-10 *"... who has saved us and called us with a holy calling, not according to our works, but according to His own purpose and grace which was given to us in Christ Jesus before time began, but has now been revealed by the appearing of our Savior Jesus Christ, who has abolished death and brought life and immortality to light through the gospel."*

Heb. 9:14 *"... how much more shall the blood of Christ, who through the eternal Spirit offered Himself without spot to God, purge your conscience from dead works to serve the living God?"*

I Pet. 1:15 *"But as He who called you is holy, you also be holy in all your conduct."*

I Pet. 2:9 *"But you are a chosen generation, a royal priesthood, a holy nation, His own special people, that you may proclaim the praises of Him who called you out of darkness into His marvelous light."*

I Pet. 5:10 *"But may the God of all grace, who called us to His eternal glory by Christ Jesus, after you have suffered a while, perfect, establish, strengthen, and settle you."*

II Pet. 1:3 *"... as His divine power has given to us all things that* *pertain to life and godliness, through the knowledge of Him who called us by glory and virtue."*

Rev. 17:14 *"These will make war with the Lamb, and the Lamb will overcome them, for He is Lord of lords and King of kings; and those who are with Him are called, chosen, and faithful."*

8. Man's salvation is *applied to him merely by the grace of God* and is not due to any inherent natural goodness or desire left in man. Salvation is entirely by the grace of God. The regenerating work of the Holy Spirit must come *before* there can be faith in the heart of man. It is this irresistible grace, as seen in the power of the Word and Holy Spirit of God, that brings man to true repentance and faith.

Is. 55:11 *"So shall My word be that goes forth from My mouth; it shall not return to Me void, but it shall accomplish what I please, and it shall prosper in the thing for which I sent it."*

Matt. 16:15-17 *"He said to them, But who do you say that I am? And Simon Peter answered and said, You are the Christ, the Son of the living God. Jesus answered and said to him, Blessed are you, Simon Bar-Jonah, for flesh and blood has not revealed this to you, but My Father who is in heaven."*

Jn. 3:27 *"John answered and said, A man can receive nothing unless it has been given to him from heaven."*

Jn. 6:44 *"No one can come to Me unless the Father who sent Me draws him; and I will raise him up at the last day."*

Jn. 6:65 *"And He said, Therefore I have said to you that no one can come to Me unless it has been granted to him by My Father."*

Jn. 17:2 *"... as You have given Him authority over all flesh, that He should give eternal life to as many as You have given Him."*

Rom. 9:16 *"So then it is not of him who wills, nor of him who runs, but of God who shows mercy."*

I Cor. 2:9-14 *"But as it is written: Eye has not seen, nor ear heard, nor have entered into the heart of man the things which God has prepared for those who love Him. But God has revealed them to us through His Spirit. For the Spirit searches all things, yes, the deep things of God. For what man knows the things of a man except the spirit of the man which is in him? Even so no one knows the things* *of God except the Spirit of God. Now we have received, not the spirit of the world, but the Spirit who is from God, that we might know the things that have been freely given to us by God. These things we also speak, not in words which man's wisdom teaches but which the Holy Spirit teaches, comparing spiritual things with spiritual. But the natural man does not receive the things of the Spirit of God, for they are foolishness to him; nor can he know them, because they are spiritually discerned."*

I Cor. 3:6-7 *"I planted, Apollos watered, but God gave the increase. So then neither he who plants is anything, nor he who waters, but God who gives the increase."*

I Cor. 4:7 *"For who makes you differ from another? And what do you have that you did not receive? Now if you did indeed receive it, why do you glory as if you had not received it?"*

Eph. 2:8-9 *"For by grace you have been saved through faith, and that not of yourselves; it is the gift of God, not of works, lest anyone should boast."*

Phil. 2:12-13 *"Therefore, my beloved, as you have always obeyed, not as in my presence only, but now much more in my absence, work out your own salvation with fear and trembling; for it is God who works in you both to will and to do for His good pleasure."*

James 1:17-18 *"Every good gift and every perfect gift is from above, and comes down from the Father of lights, with whom there is no variation or shadow of turning. Of His own will He brought us forth by the word of truth, that we might be a kind of firstfruits of His creatures."*

I Jn. 5:20 *"And we know that the Son of God has come and has given us an understanding, that we may know Him who is true; and we are in Him who is true, in His Son Jesus Christ. This is the true God and eternal life."*

QUESTIONS:

1. Why is it that the preaching of the gospel is called *"foolishness"* in I Corinthians 1:18,21, and 22?

2. In I Corinthians 2, where does Paul refer to the external call of the gospel, and where does he refer to the internal call of the gospel?

3. If we are going to explain the fact that God's grace through His Holy Spirit is irresistible, where must we begin? and why?

4. Give three texts that you feel are best to explain the doctrine of irresistible grace, and explain why you chose them.

5. Unbelievers do resist the preaching of the gospel. Does this deny the doctrine which says that the grace of God is irresistible? Explain:

6. What will surely cause the preaching of the gospel to be "successful"?

7. List some of the key passages you would use if you were going to explain this doctrine of *irresistible grace* to someone who had not heard it before.

16

The Doctrine of the
Perseverance of the Saints
Part 1

Totally depraved man who is chosen by God unto salvation, redeemed by the atoning blood of Jesus, and brought to faith by the irresistible operation of the Holy Spirit, is also *kept in the faith unto everlasting life* by the power of God. This is the doctrine which is called the *perseverance of the saints.*

Preservation and Perseverance

The commonly used title of this point of Calvinism should not confuse us – especially the word "perseverance. It is *not* the work of the saints under their own power who bring about this perseverance in the faith, but it is the work of God. Some prefer to use the word *"preservation"* of the saints.

We can make an important distinction here. The saints actually do *"persevere"* in the faith. They are very much active in sanctification. Phil. 2:12, 13 explains the balance between man's responsibility and God's enabling power. *"Therefore, my beloved, as you have always obeyed, not as in my presence only, but now much more in my absence, work out your own salvation with fear and trembling; for it is God who works in you both to will and to do for His good pleasure."* (*cf.* also II Tim. 2:19; Titus 3:5-8)

But it is God who *"preserves"* Christians and keeps them

from ultimately falling into perdition. I Pet. 1:3-5 clearly teaches, *"Blessed be the God and Father of our Lord Jesus Christ, who according to His abundant mercy has begotten us again to a living hope through the resurrection of Jesus Christ from the dead, to an inheritance incorruptible and undefiled and that does not fade away, reserved in heaven for you, who are kept by the power of God through faith for salvation ready to be revealed in the last time."*

I John 5:18 states in the NKJV, *"We know that whoever is born of God does not sin; but he who has been born of God keeps himself, and the wicked one does not touch him."* It might appear from this verse that the believer must "keep himself" in the faith. There is a variant reading of the word "himself" in the Greek that I believe is more accurate. Instead of "himself" the word is "him" (in the Greek manuscripts, there is a one letter difference which causes this change). The reading should be something like we find in the New International Version (and also the New American Standard Version), *"We know that anyone born of God does not continue to sin; the one who was born of God keeps him safe, and the evil one cannot harm him."* In these translations, the subject of the sentence is not man, but Christ ("the one who was born of God"). It is Christ who keeps the believer safe from the Devil, not man himself. Even if the NKJV translation is correct, it is saying that man must persevere, but it does not eliminate the preservation by God.

The beauty of this doctrine is how God sovereignly works within His elect people, preserving them and causing them to persevere unto the end. It is God who has removed all dominion of sin from His people (Rom. 6:14) and He indwells and dominates their hearts and wills so that their desire is to daily repent and believe in the Lord Jesus Christ, trusting His promise that all who believe have *"everlasting life"* (as opposed to a temporary life with hopes of making it to everlasting life). When the Bible uses the word "everlasting," that is exactly what it means (cf. John 3:36; 6:47).

Preservation and perseverance are not in conflict, but they actually are the two aspects of the same doctrine by which God saves. It is God who *preserves His elect people by causing them to persevere in the faith.*

The Arminian Position

The doctrine taught by the Arminians is consistent with their previous teachings on the matter of salvation. As are their other doctrines, it is centered and *dependant on the work of man*. According to them, man is not completely dead in sin and he can choose by himself to be saved. It then follows that he could also lose that salvation due to his own weakness and bad choices.

In their system, someone whose sins are atoned for and who is born again could lose that faith and ultimately go to hell. As long as he remains faithful, all is well. But it is up to man, by his own free will, to hold on to his faith without which no one can be saved.

Herein lies the danger of a man-centered religion. There can be *no comfort, no assurance, and no complete and abiding joy* since all might be lost when a man falls from "true faith" back into unbelief. What this says is that saving grace is not *abiding grace*. The indwelling of the Holy Spirit is not an *abiding presence* (because man can always "resist" this power even after the Holy Spirit has come to man). Notice how different this teaching is from that of Jesus in John 14:16, *"And I will pray the Father, and He will give you another Helper, that He may abide with you forever."*

Romans 7 and the Struggle of the Christian

The picture presented by Arminianism is of someone who is "in and out" of salvation with the hope that at death they will be "in." Much of the assurance of salvation depends on the ability of man.

It is natural that the Arminian would interpret Romans chapter 7:15-25 as speaking of the unregenerate state of man instead of the struggles of man as a Christian. The Arminian is wrong at this point. Paul clearly states that he sins even as a regenerated person (*cf.* v. 22 – the use of the term, *"the inward man,"* which indicates the new nature in Paul), *"For what I am doing, I do not understand. For what I will to do, that I do not practice; but what I hate, that I do. For the good that I will to do, I do not do; but the evil I will not to do, that I practice."* (Rom. 7:15, 19) Paul is not saying here that he loses his salvation or gains it back at any time. He is simply saying that even as a believer, sin still clings to him and he falls into it. *"But now, it is no longer I who do it, but sin that dwells in me. Now if I do what I will not to do, it is no longer I who do it, but sin that dwells in me."* (Romans 7:17, 20) The real *"I"* is Paul's new nature in Christ. But the sin that continues to dwell in him is the old nature of Adam that clings to all of us as long as we dwell in this world.

Such sin as Paul refers to in Romans 7 would condemn any man – even the least sin against any of the commandments of God would be sufficient to condemn (as Paul alludes to in 7:24, *"O wretched man that I am! Who will deliver me from this body of death?"*). We would perish if it were not for the grace of God who has given us His Holy Spirit who works repentance in us. Romans 8:1 fittingly belongs to the conclusion of Romans 7 which says, *"I thank God – through Jesus Christ our Lord! So then, with the mind I myself serve the law of God, but with the flesh the law of sin. There is therefore now no condemnation to those who are in Christ Jesus, who do not walk according to the flesh, but according to the Spirit."* (Romans 7:25, 8:1) In *The Canons of Dort*, Fifth Head of Doctrine, Article 1, we read, *"Those whom God, according to His purpose, calls to the communion of His Son, our Lord Jesus Christ, and regenerates by His Holy Spirit, He also delivers from the dominion and slavery of sin, though in this life He does not deliver them altogether from the body of sin and from the infirmities of the flesh."*

As we observe the excruciating agony of Paul's struggle (or as we look at the struggles with sin in our own lives) what a comfort it is to realize that the outcome of this struggle is never left in doubt for those who are "in Christ Jesus, who do not walk according to the flesh, but according to the Spirit". The *"flesh"* here refers to the old nature in Adam that once enslaved and dominated us. That nature is gone, along with the curse that accompanied it. Now the Holy Spirit of God dwells in us – the very one who has made us *"new creatures"* (see II Cor. 5:16-17).

It should be noted that there is intense opposition to this most comforting doctrine by the Arminians who base salvation on the sovereignty of man. As one TV evangelist once said, 'Calvinism is born in the pits of hell... and has condemned thousands to hell.' The basis for this and other statements contrary to this doctrine rests on a total misunderstanding of the foundation for it – God's eternal elective decrees. Calvinism is often falsely depicted as teaching a doctrine that once chosen for salvation, one can sin with abandon and still be saved. Nowhere does it teach this! What it does teach is that God will bring His erring child back to Himself, by way of repentance.

In the position of the Arminians, one has to be "re-saved" each time he falls into some sin (it usually has to be some very grievous sin, rather than just one of the daily sins of man). Often missing in Arminian thought is the doctrine of the active obedience of Christ which is His righteousness imputed to the believer.

According to their doctrine of man's free will, faith can be lost, regained, and lost again. Missing is the *assurance* of a sovereign God who will not lose His sheep. Once He gives His Holy Spirit, he does not withdraw Him from His people, so that they plunge themselves into everlasting destruction. This God-given assurance comes from the promises of God revealed in His Word, the testimony of the indwelling Spirit assuring us that we are heirs (Rom. 8:16), and from a serious and holy desire to preserve a good conscience (*Canons of Dort,* Fifth Head of Doctrine, Article 10).

According to the thinking of Arminians, this doctrine of Calvinism gives the believer a *license to sin* without any worry that he might lose his salvation. That temptation does exist, but it is foreign to Calvinistic teaching. Such an argument is ridiculous, as Paul says in Romans 6:1, 2 *"What shall we say then? Shall we continue in sin that grace may abound? Certainly not! How shall we who died to sin live any longer in it?"* No Christian would ever think that he is free to sin just because he is saved and preserved in his salvation by the grace and power of God. In Galatians, the Apostle Paul taught what real freedom is – to be redeemed by Jesus' blood. Here he warns believers: *"Stand fast therefore in the liberty by which Christ has made us free, and do not be entangled again with a yoke of bondage. For you, brethren, have been called to liberty; only do not use liberty as an opportunity for the flesh, but through love serve one another."* (Gal. 5:1, 13)

The Arminian does admit that God *makes available* the power to persevere, but it is entirely up to man whether he chooses to use this power and persevere or whether he will reject it. The bottom line is always the "free" will and the "free" choice of man.

The "Saints"

The reference to the "saints" should be explained. These are not special, deceased people who are singled out of Christendom because of some extraordinary works they performed and therefore were given the title of "saint" by the church. That is the Roman Catholic concept of saints.

When the Bible uses the word *"saints,"* it is another way of referring to God's elect people. The word *"saint"* comes from the Latin word *"sanctus"* which means *"holy."* In the Greek also where the word *"saint"* appears, it is the word *"hagios"* which also means *"holy"* (see Phil. 4:21; II Thess. 1:10). The word *"saint"* is also the root in the word *"sanctification"* which means to be *cleansed (made holy) and separated unto God to do His will.* This is what is meant when the Bible refers to believers as *"saints."*

Those whom God has, by His grace, cleansed, remain cleansed from sin. This does not mean that man does not need to put sin to death in his life or can be careless about it. We struggle with temptation and sin all our life long. By God's grace we recognize our sin and turn to God. I Cor. 10:13 says, *"No temptation has overtaken you except such as is common to man; but God is faithful, who will not allow you to be tempted beyond what you are able, but with the temptation will also make the way of escape, that you may be able to bear it."* It is God, through His Word and Holy Spirit, who continually works repentance in His elect and it is God who promises that all who confess their sins will be forgiven. *"If we confess our sins, He is faithful and just to forgive us our sins and to cleanse us from all unrighteousness."* (1 John 1:9)

A Glorious Doctrine

This doctrine is especially glorious in view of the fact that if it were left to man to maintain his faith by his own power, he would surely fall completely away in a moment. Only a biblical view of God, of man, and of man's sin can result in a proper understanding of the power it takes – the absolute, sovereign power of God – to give us victory over sin. To be sure, the matter of assurance of salvation is not easy for us to accept as it is explained in the words of *Heidelberg Catechism* Q. 60 "...*although my conscience accuses me*, that I have grievously sinned against all the commandments of God, and have never kept any of them, and am still prone always to all evil, yet God, without any merit of mine, of mere grace, grants and imputes to me the perfect satisfaction, righteousness, and holiness of Christ, as if I had never had nor committed any sins, and had myself accomplished all the obedience which Christ has fulfilled for me; *if only I accept such a benefit with a believing heart*." Constantly, the Christian's prayer must be, *"Lord, I believe, help my unbelief!"* (Mark 9:24) Once God has imputed the righteousness of Christ to His people, He does not remove it again due to an error in judgment on His part or due to the failure of man to cling to it.

This doctrine of perseverance is inseparably tied to the entire plan of God's salvation (see *Canons of Dort*, Chapter 5, Article 1). The simple truth is that nobody, and no power whatever, can undo what God, from eternity, has determined to do. God does not write the names of His elect in the Book of Life before the foundation of the world with an eraser in hand!

The Christian is painfully aware of his failures and how he daily breaks all the commandments of God. Should this cause him to doubt his salvation? Or, should the basis of assurance rest alone on his good obedience and faithfulness? No, neither of these! It is God who is able to keep that which we have committed unto him – the salvation of our souls – unto the coming of Jesus and everlasting life. *"Nevertheless I am not ashamed: for I know whom I have believed, and am persuaded that he is able to keep that which I have committed unto him against that day."* (II Tim. 1:12) Likewise Peter says that believers are *"kept by the power of God through faith for salvation ready to be revealed in the last time."* (I Pet. 1:5)

It is not in our own righteousness that we as believers will stand on the judgment day, but in the imputed righteousness of Christ which is ours by faith. If, after faith in Christ, we place our hope of salvation in our works, we deny the righteousness of Christ. Notice that this was the sin of the Galatian church that Paul is warning about:

"Are you so foolish? Having begun in the Spirit, are you now being made perfect by the flesh?" (Gal. 3:3) Even our best righteousness is insufficient to save us, and even more frightening is that our best righteousness is sufficient to condemn us. Is. 64:6 tells us, *"But we are all like an unclean thing, and all our righteousnesses are like filthy rags; we all fade as a leaf, and our iniquities, like the wind, have taken us away."* It is exclusively in the righteousness of Jesus Christ that we have the assurance of salvation and life. This is imputed to all who call on the Lord Jesus Christ in true faith. It is the unbeliever who will stand dressed in his own filthy rags of unrighteousness, and be cast from the wedding feast into everlasting condemnation (see Matt. 22:11-14).

God is the Preserver of the Faith and the Faithful

It is our sovereign, covenant God who preserves His people. This preservation does not begin only at the point when man becomes a Christian. It *began before the foundation of the world* when all of God's redemptive purpose was laid out – when the fall of our first parents Adam and Eve was ordained, when man was elected, and when Christ was foreordained to be the Savior. It was before the foundation of the world that God entered the names of the saved into the "Book of Life." God does not have to amend the list of names because man has frustrated His sovereign will nor does he have to wait on man before he can finalize the Book of Life at Christ's return.

All of history displays the preservation and unfolding of God's redemptive plan and purpose. The people of God are the focus of this plan – the apple of God's eye. They are cared for and preserved in miraculous ways. God does not give His people the promise of everlasting life (*cf.* John 3:16) only to take it away because of man's weakness or unwillingness. God's plan is not a failure because it is overthrown by any of the enemies of God and man – the devil, the world, and our own flesh. If man were left to himself without the power to persevere, all would perish. It is unthinkable that God would have Jesus shed His blood in vain for anyone.

The Assurance of Salvation

It must be understood that it is God who gives us true faith.

"For by grace you have been saved through faith, and that not of yourselves; it is the gift of God." (Eph. 2:8) This is the ground for our assurance of salvation. The *Heidelberg Catechism* speaks in Question 54 concerning membership in the "Holy Catholic Church" (the elect Church of God) and says, *"and that I am and forever shall remain a living member of this communion."* It is also Question 1 which says, *"Wherefore, by His Holy Spirit, He also assures me of eternal life...."*

For there to be true assurance of salvation, there must be a firm and true faith in what God has revealed to us in His Holy Word. It is God who has worked this faith in us through His Holy Spirit. We dare not base this assurance on anything taught outside the Bible (such as the superstitions or the traditions of men). The reason that the Pietism which followed closely on the heals of the Reformation lost its doctrine of assurance was that they sought it outside of the Word of God, outside of the grace of God, and outside of the finished and imputed work of Christ.

Certainly we can say that *"we are assured of our faith by the works thereof"* (*Heidelberg Catechism* Q. 86). Works alone can not bring assurance. *They must be works of faith in accordance with the Scriptures.* The works which we perform are the works of God in and through us. Isaiah 26:12 says, *"LORD, You will establish peace for us, for You have also done all our works in us."* Notice how the Apostle Paul brings out this fact in the comforting passage from II Corinthians 5:1-7, *"For we know that if our earthly house, this tent, is destroyed, we have a building from God, a house not made with hands, eternal in the heavens. For in this we groan, earnestly desiring to be clothed with our habitation which is from heaven, if indeed, having been clothed, we shall not be found naked. For we who are in this tent groan, being burdened, not because we want to be unclothed, but further clothed, that mortality may be swallowed up by life. **Now He who has prepared us for this very thing is God, who also has given us the Spirit as a guarantee.** Therefore we are **always confident**, knowing that while we are at home in the body we are absent from the Lord. For we walk by faith, not by sight."* (Emphasis mine)

We see this relationship between true faith and true works when we see the faithfulness of Abraham according to James 2:22, 23

"Do you see that faith was working together with his works, and by works faith was made perfect? And the Scripture was fulfilled which says, Abraham believed God, and it was accounted to him for righteousness. And he was called the friend of God." And perhaps the most clear teaching on this relationship is seen in John 3:21, *"But he who does the truth comes to the light, that his deeds may be clearly seen, that **they have been done in God.**"* (Emphasis mine)

Without question, men fall into sin each day – as they have done ever since the Fall. Yet, God is merciful, and has promised that he will not impute our transgressions unto us. First, we read in Psalm 130:3, 4 *If You, LORD, should mark iniquities, O Lord, who could stand? But there is forgiveness with You, That You may be feared."* If God would add our daily sins to our charge we could not stand a moment because of His just judgment. However, God imputes the righteousness of Christ to us, and not our iniquities. Psalm 32: 1, 2 says, *"Blessed is he whose transgression is forgiven, Whose sin is covered. Blessed is the man to whom the LORD does not impute iniquity, And in whose spirit there is no guile."*

Also we find the New Testament abounding in references to the imputed righteousness of Christ as our righteousness that can stand before God. This righteousness is not *un*-imputed when a true believer falls into sin. On the contrary, it is the righteousness of Christ which covers our sins in the sight of God. II Corinthians 5:19 and 21 teach us, *"... that God was in Christ reconciling the world to Himself, not imputing their trespasses to them, and has committed to us the word of reconciliation. For He made Him who knew no sin to be sin for us, that we might become the righteousness of God in Him."* I John 2:1 tells us that the sinner has the righteous Christ to look to when he sins, *"My little children, these things I write to you, that you may not sin. And if anyone sins, we have an Advocate with the Father, Jesus Christ the righteous."* See Hebrews 2:17-18 and 4:14-16.

It is by the testimony of the Holy Spirit within us that God assures us that our whole salvation rests in Christ's blood and righteousness (cf. *Heidelberg Catechism* Q. 56). Romans 8:16 says, *"The Spirit Himself bears witness with our spirit that we are children of God,"* The very presence of the Holy Spirit within us testifies to us and assures us of our adoption and the inheritance that goes with it – everlasting life (see Romans 8:14-18 and II Tim. 1:7-9). We will never be put up for re-adoption at some later date. I John 3:9 speaks of the believer not sinning a sin which is unto death (condemnation), *"Whoever has been born of God does not sin, for His seed remains in him; and he cannot sin, because he has been born of God."*

Again I John 3:19-24 tells us of the relationship between our works of love and the Holy Spirit residing in us. It is the Holy Spirit dwelling in our hearts who produces these good works which also assure our hearts. *"And by this we know that we are of the truth, and shall assure our hearts before Him. For if our heart condemns us, God is greater than our heart, and knows all things. Beloved, if our heart does not condemn us, we have confidence toward God. And whatever we ask we receive from Him, because we keep His commandments and do those things that are pleasing in His sight. And this is His commandment: that we should believe on the name of His Son Jesus Christ and love one another, as He gave us commandment. Now he who keeps His commandments abides in Him, and He in him. And by this we know that He abides in us, by the Spirit whom He has given us."*

Our salvation rests in the propitiation for our sins and the imputed righteousness of Christ. It is God who, through His Word and Spirit creates in us the faith to believe this and the assurance that it is ours forever. These acts of God are both complete and irrevocable.

In the next lesson we will look at the matter of backsliding in relation to perseverance.

QUESTIONS:

1. What is the difference between "preservation" and "perseverance" in regard to this doctrine?

2. How is this doctrine related to the other four points of Calvinism?

3. Why do some people have such strong opposition to this doctrine?

   • What do they often claim that this doctrine leads to?

4. What is the Arminian position concerning the matter of "persever-

ance"?

- Why does their teaching not lead to assurance?

5. What is the basis upon which the doctrine of the "perseverance of the saints" rests.

- What is the ground of our assurance of salvation?

6. What comfort does the Christian have when he falls into sin?

- Is Romans 7 speaking about the struggle with sin in the life of the believer or the unbeliever?

- Why is this important to know?

7. What part does the Holy Spirit play in the matter of our assurance of salvation?

8. Who are "saints" according to the Bible?

- What does this word mean?

- How did they get to be saints?

17

The Doctrine of the
Perseverance of the Saints
Part 2

"The carnal mind is unable to comprehend this doctrine of the perseverance of the saints and the certainty thereof... Satan abhors it, the world ridicules it, the ignorant and hypocritical abuse it, and the heretics oppose it. But the bride of Christ has always most tenderly loved and constantly defended it as an inestimable treasure...." (*Canons of Dort*, Fifth Head of Doctrine, Article 15)

Not only is this doctrine impossible for the unregenerate to comprehend, but it is often confused in the mind of the regenerate as well. Let us look at some of these difficulties.

Backsliding

The doctrine of the *perseverance of the saints* does not teach that Christians never fall into sin. Christians do sin and they "backslide" to various degrees. We should understand what we mean by "backslide." We are not to interpret this as a sin that needs no repentance, as though "backsliding" is something other than a sin and can even be tolerated. On the contrary, *the sin of backsliding is one that calls for heartfelt repentance* as we see with the saints in the Scripture (*cf.* David's and Peter's confessions).

Backsliding is not a falling away completely from the faith or the state of grace into which God has placed the believer. Some sins are so grievous that it might appear that a person has departed from the faith completely and has never been regenerated. We might think of it as a child who may wander morally far from his parents. He may seek to depart from the love of his parents. But the parents have not ceased to love the child. In the case of our heavenly Father, he will continue to love His children and to work repentance in them so that they will return to Him in repentance and faith. Recall the parable of the Prodigal Son from Luke 15.

The *Canons of Dort* state in the Fifth Head of Doctrine, Articles 6 and 7 *"But God, who is rich in mercy, according to His unchangeable purpose of election, does not wholly withdraw the Holy Spirit from His own people even in their grievous falls; nor suffers them to proceed so far as to lose the grace of adoption and forfeit the state of justification, or to commit the sin unto death or against the Holy Spirit; nor does He permit them to be totally deserted, and to plunge themselves into everlasting destruction. For in the first place, in these falls He preserves in them the incorruptible seed of regeneration from perishing or being totally lost; and again, by His Word and Spirit He certainly and effectually renews them to repentance, to a sincere and godly sorrow for theirs sins...."*

God may allow the saints to fall very deeply into sins before he brings them back through loving chastisement. The purpose of this is that they will have learned a valuable lesson which *"renders them much more careful and solicitous to continue in the ways of the Lord, which He has ordained, that they who walk therein may keep the assurance of persevering."* (*Canons of Dort*, 5th Head of Doctrine, Article 13)

The return from a period of backsliding into sin is entirely by the grace of God who draws them unto Himself in repentance and renewed faith. The *Canons of Dort* put it this way: *"Thus it is not in consequence of their own merits or strength, but of God's free mercy, that they neither totally fall from faith and grace nor continue and perish finally in their backslidings...."* (*Canons of Dort*, Fifth Head of Doctrine, Article 8)

Passages Cited by Arminians

The Arminian rejects the idea of "backsliding" *within* the faith. Rather, he would say that a person has fallen out of the faith and the grace of God. There are two Scripture passages in particular which they refer to in order to substantiate their position are Hebrews 6:4-6 and Galatians 5:4.

Hebrews 6:4-6 says: *"For it is impossible for those who were once enlightened, and have tasted the heavenly gift, and have become partakers of the Holy Spirit, and have tasted the good word of God and the powers of the age to come, if they fall away, to renew them again to repentance, since they crucify again for themselves the Son of God, and put Him to an open shame."* On the surface it may appear to say that Christians can lose their salvation, but it does not.

First, all Scripture must be seen in its context. The broad context is the whole Bible which in so many places, as we shall see later, presents to us the comfort that nothing can separate us from the love of God in Jesus Christ (Rom. 8:31-39; see *Heidelberg Catechism* Q. 28 "no creature shall separate us from His love, since all creatures are so in His hand, that without His will they cannot so much as move.") The Scriptures are never contradictory. The overwhelming evidence of Scripture legislates against an interpretation which suggests that a Christian, once saved, could ever lose that salvation.

Secondly, we need to take this passage in the context of what the writer of Hebrews had been teaching previously. In chapters 3 and 4 we are taught about the Israelites who enjoyed the blessings of the covenant with God, who were instructed concerning the Promised Land, who were fed and guided through the wilderness, yet, who did not trust God (Heb. 3:7-11). In addition, Heb. 3:12 speaks of these Israelites as having *"an evil heart of unbelief."* The writer of Hebrews warns his hearers not to enjoy the covenant blessings (as the Jews had done), but fail to trust in God with true faith. Just as the Israelites without faith could not enter the Promised Land, but perished in the wilderness, so too, the covenant people he was writing to would not enter the Promised Land of heaven if they did not believe in God's salvation through Jesus Christ. To be numbered among the Covenant people of God does not guarantee salvation, but it guarantees them the promise of salvation if they believe.

Again Heb. 3:14 says, *"For we have become partakers of Christ if we hold the beginning of our confidence steadfast to the end."* The *proof* that we are partakers of Christ rests on whether or not we remain faithful (contrast also Heb. 4:3, 6; see also I Jn. 2:19) This is different from saying that we actually are partakers of Christ and then lose it in the end. Many within God's covenant enjoy the promises, and yet do not believe them. *"But it is not that the word of God has taken no effect. For they are not all Israel who are of Israel...."* (Rom. 9:6)

In Chapter 5 the writer is telling the people that Christ is a priest after the order of Melchizedek (vv. 6-10), rather than a priest after the order of the Levitical priesthood. It was because of their lack of faith that they still could not grasp this truth, choosing rather to follow the Old Testament ceremonial laws. The writer would like to give them some meaty teaching, but he could not because of they were *"dull of hearing"* and *"unskilled in the word of righteousness."* Therefore he must still give them *"milk, and not of solid food."* (5:12-14)

Finally, we must look carefully at the words used in this passage. These professing Hebrew Christians were in the danger of being led away by Jewish heresies. They had all the background of the covenant, they were included in the covenant of their fathers and therefore were *"enlightened,"* and had *"tasted of the heavenly gifts,"* and were *"made partakers of the Holy Spirit."* What the writer is saying is that these Jews had been influenced by the covenant blessings of God (*"tasted"*) but were not partakers of them in faith. The presence of God's Spirit was with them, yet not in them. If they did not partake of the covenant promises in faith, but *"fell away"* from them and remained in unbelief, it would be impossible for them to be restored by repentance once God's judgment was passed (as in the case of the Israelites who had to perish in the wilderness). If the Hebrews rejected the promise of God in Jesus Christ there would be no other savior – they would be guilty of crucifying the Son of God again and bringing shame on Him.

The Arminians, in using this passage to prove that it is possible to fall away, may being saying more than they want to. You notice also that if the hearers of this Epistle to the Hebrews fall away, as Arminians teach, it is *"impossible to renew them again unto repentance."* This they do not teach (*ie.* once fallen away, always fallen away). They teach that one could be a regenerated believer, fall away, and then be regenerated again. If they interpret this as saying that the Holy Spirit could depart from a person, they would also be forced to say that such a person could never again be saved. One of the early church fathers, Tertullian (in his book, *Homily on Baptism*) consistently taught that if anyone sinned after being baptized, he could never again be saved. He was wrong in this, but is more consistently wrong than the Arminian of today.

The other passage often used by Arminians to teach that the regenerated person may be lost again is Galatians 5:4 which says, *"You have become estranged from Christ, you who attempt to be justified by law; you have fallen from grace."*

The context will help us again. Paul is writing to the Galatians who had been taught the true gospel, but were now in danger of leaving that teaching and reverting to the false teaching of a justification by works (Gal. 3:1-3). Gal. 4:9 warns against turning to the law as a way of justification (ie. *"weak and beggarly elements"*) and says that these people did not actually *"know God"* in true faith, but were more realistically *"known of God."* Paul is simply teaching in Gal. 5:4 that if you follow a doctrine of being justified by the law, you automatically depart from a doctrine that teaches us that we are justified by grace through faith. One may know of God without *truly knowing* God by true faith. Anyone who commits that error is not entitled to say that they are under the grace of God, rather they are fallen away from it.

"Once saved, Always Saved?"

This term is often used by both Calvinists and Arminians in reference to salvation. When it is understood properly it can certainly be a true statement. Yet, if two diametrically opposed systems of doctrine teach the same thing, there must be a different understanding in the meaning of the statement.

This is true in this case. The key lies in the word *"saved."*

Dispensationalism, championed by Scofield, teaches that Christ can be your Savior without being your Lord. When you fall away, you are falling away from the "Lordship" of Jesus, and not necessarily from the salvation.

Scofield differentiates Christians as being "spiritual" and "carnal" Christians. "Carnal Christians" do not yield to the Lordship of Christ, but he can still be their Savior. This is his explanation on the teaching of I Cor. 2:14. One must wonder how such an error can be reconciled with the teaching of Romans 8. Romans 8:5 says, *"For those who live according to the flesh set their minds on the things of the flesh, but those who live according to the Spirit, the things of the Spirit."* It is a serious error to take Paul's teaching in Romans 8 to teach that there are two kinds of Christians – those who are "carnal" and those who are "spiritual." In fact, what Paul is teaching is precisely the opposite. To be "carnal" leads to death, while the Spirit gives life. *"For to be carnally minded is death, but to be spiritually minded is life and peace. Because the carnal mind is enmity against God; for it is not subject to the law of God, nor indeed can be."* (Rom. 8:6-7) Paul is not describing two categories of Christians, but that there is an *antithesis* (a direct and all-pervading distinction) between believers (living by the Spirit) and unbelievers (living by the flesh).

It is simply an impossibility to have Jesus as your *Savior* and not at the same time have Him as your *Lord*. This is what Jesus is referring to in Luke 6:46, *"But why do you call Me 'Lord, Lord,' and do not do the things which I say?"* Those who use the term "Lord", but who do not submit to Jesus as Savior and Lord are lost. Jesus becomes our Lord by virtue of the fact that He bought us with His precious blood, and owns us, body and soul, in life and in death. If he is your savior, then He is your Lord. Our *submission* to His Lordship should grow throughout our life.

To believe in Jesus as your Savior means that you have also denied yourself, taken up the cross, and followed Jesus (cf. Matt. 16:24). A follower of Jesus has yielded to His Lordship. A denial of self must also include a denial of all innate power that a sinful person might have and complete submission to Jesus Christ. Paul refers to this in Romans 10:9, *"That if you confess with your mouth the Lord*

Jesus and believe in your heart that God has raised Him from the dead, you will be saved. " The first half of this verse teaches the confession that believers make. The second half refers to the risen Lord whom we must believe and follow from our heart (out of which all of our life flows).

Backsliding and Church Discipline

All Christians fall into sin. Sin itself is not the ground for church discipline, but failure to repent of sin. However, not all Christians who fall into sin immediately *repent of their sin.* They may continue to commit the same sin for some time. It is for this latter group that church discipline must be exercised.

The Canons of Dort, Fifth Head of Doctrine, Article 14 states, *"And as it has pleased God, by the preaching of the gospel, to begin this work of grace in us, so He preserves, continues, and perfects it by the hearing and reading of His Word, by meditation thereon, and by the exhortations, threatenings, and promises thereof, and by the use of the sacraments."*

God uses various means to cause His people to persevere. Internally, he pricks our conscience by His Word and Holy Spirit. In a more external way, when professing Christians fall into sin and do not turn from it, God has given the church authority, through its elders, to exercise Christian discipline. In that way, discipline serves as one facet of this doctrine of the perseverance of the saints.

While mere men cannot know the heart of man in any exhaustive way, but only by his actions, the church must attempt to *restore* all those who profess to be Christians and fall away from the truth and godly living. That is the purpose of discipline – the *restoration of the wandering* (see I Cor. 5:5). It is done out of love – love for God and concern for His righteousness, and love for man and concern for his godliness.

Heidelberg Catechism Q. 85 explains, among church members, how the kingdom of heaven is shut and opened by Christian discipline. Christian discipline involves admonition by fellow Christians and by the elders of the Church. The course of action taken in discipline is helpful in understanding this connection with perseverance. An erring Christian is first *admonished* (warned) concerning the sin and told that it must be repented of and, therefore, cease. If there is still no repentance, the next step is to *suspend* this person from the Lord's table since by his life the person is declaring or exhibiting that he is not in communion with God or His people. This is a most serious and final warning. If there is still not repentance the sinning person must be *excommunicated* from the church. This means that he is considered and declared to be a heathen and outside of the Church or outside of the Christian faith. The church is not condemning him to hell, but declaring that as long as the person remains unrepentant and shows none of the fruits of faith, he is lost and is to be treated like an unbeliever.

Throughout this process, the desire is always that the unrepentant sinner will repent. If the Holy Spirit is in this person, he will ultimately repent and be happily restored to full communion in the church.

But, what if the person does not repent and remains such unto death? Does this mean that a person who was once a Christian has now lost his salvation? Not at all. It does say that the person who once professed to be a Christian was lying and has never been a Christian. This is what John is teaching in I John 2:19 where it refers to such a case, *"They went out from us, but they were not of us; for if they had been of us, they would have continued with us; but they went out that they might be made manifest, that none of them were of us."*

Certainly Christians who claim to believe in the doctrine of the *perseverance of the saints* must be faithful to exercise Christian discipline in the Church, recognizing that this is a tool by which God preserves His church and causes His people to persevere (see Hebrews 12:5-15). Failure to exercise Christian discipline when church members sin is to relinquish one of the primary means whereby God preserves His saints.

There are No Hypocritical "Christians"

There are Christians and there are hypocrites. There are no Christian hypocrites in the real sense of the word. A hypocrite is a pretender. He says he is a Christian, when in fact he is not. A hypocrite is not just an inconsistent Christian or a sinning Christian. *Whenever the Bible uses the term "hypocrite" it is used of those who are outside of Christ, but act like they are right with God.*

This is not to say that Christians never act *inconsistently* with their faith. They do this every time they sin. They do this every day. But, the Christian is not pretending to be a believer when in fact he is not. When we read references in the Bible to "hypocrites" and the condemnation that is theirs (cf. Matthew 23), we should not think that these refer to sinning Christians. They were people pretending to be believers.

A clear differentiation between the true Christian, the hypocrite, and the clearly heathen is seen in the parable of the sower (Matthew 13). In that parable Jesus taught that the seed of the Word was rejected completely in the lives of some. In others the seed *appeared to take root*, but was short-lived and never produced the fruit of faith. Finally, there was seed that fell on the fertile heart, took root, and produced the fruits of faith.

According to this, did true believers fail to be saved in the end, as the seed which began to sprout but was either withered or choked out? As Jesus explains the parable, we can see that this was never the case. Where the seed *appeared outwardly* to grow for a while and then died there was never the fruit of God's grace – true faith. This group could best be placed in the category of the "hypocrite" since there was, for a short time, the *appearance* of faith, but with no fruits or continued life.

Take the Bible for What it Says

The easiest way to see this doctrine as it is taught in the Bible is to simply take the Bible at face value. We might easily read right over some of the most precious truths concerning the certainty and continuity of our salvation. In the next lesson we will look at many of the passages that teach this doctrine, but for now we must be reminded of the importance of *how* we must read them.

When the Bible says that we *"have everlasting life"* that is precisely what it means. *"Everlasting"* refers to something that has no end. God does not give us a temporary salvation or only a temporal life in Christ. When the Bible says that the believer *will not perish* it means just that.

The Bible does not use the *future tense* in regard to having salvation as though we will have to wait and see if it works out, or if we will perhaps fall away before we actually possess it. The Bible may refer to the future as the perfection or the completion of our salvation. But, it does not leave it in doubt. At the moment that a Christian believes, he *has* everlasting life. He has the beginning of it and is in possession of it *now*.

I John 3:2 says, *"Beloved, now we are children of God; and it has not yet been revealed what we shall be, but we know that when He is revealed, we shall be like Him, for we shall see Him as He is.* Just notice the certainties here: *"now are we..."; "shall be..."; "shall see...."* These words are present realities even though there is a more glorious life to come.

Conclusion

The doctrine of the *perseverance of the saints* is inseparable with the other points of Calvinism. It cannot stand alone, but is dependant on the sovereign grace and power of God as we have already studied.

The other four doctrines cannot stand without this doctrine. If God has sovereignly ordered our whole salvation, then He too will maintain it and preserve us in it forever. Since God is almighty He is able to do all His holy will, and willing also, being a faithful Father.

"And I give them eternal life, and they shall never perish; neither shall anyone snatch them out of My hand. My Father, who has given them to Me, is greater than all; and no one is able to snatch them out of My Father's hand. I and My Father are one." (John 10:28-30)

Questions:

1. What is meant by "backsliding"?

   • What is *not* meant when we refer to "backsliding"?

2. What purpose does God have in allowing Christians to backslide in their faith?

 • What tools does God use to restore them?

3. According to Hebrews 6:4-6, does a Christian lose his salvation?

 • Explain your answer from the context of this passage.

4. What does "fallen from grace" mean in Galatians 5:4?

5. What do some people mean by the expression "carnal Christian"?

 • What is the error in this expression?

 • Explain why a Christian must always have Jesus as both Savior and Lord?

6. Complete this statement: Christian discipline in the church is for those who...

 • Do Christians ever get excommunicated from the church and become restored again?   Explain:

 • What does I John 2:19 say about those who leave the church or are excommunicated and never return?

7. What is the connection between Christian discipline by the Church and the doctrine of perseverance of the saints?

8. The Christian who does not live in accord with the Christian faith is a "hypocritical Christian." TRUE FALSE Explain:

 • How does the parable of the Sower help us in understanding the doctrine of the perseverance of the saints?

9. Give some examples of where "taking the Bible for what it says" helps us to see this doctrine properly.

 • When does "everlasting life" begin for a Christian?

 • Prove your answer from the Bible.

 • When does everlasting life end?

 • Prove your answer from the Bible.

10. Explain the importance of understanding every Bible passage in its "context."

18

The Doctrine of the Perseverance of the Saints Part 3

The Scriptures abound with references concerning the certainty of our salvation which God has given us in His sovereign grace. This should not surprise us since the Bible is unified in its message that man's salvation is totally in the power of God and is the work of His grace in us.

Our God is a merciful God who continually *comforts us in our faith by assuring believers of their security.* The God who has chosen us, redeemed us and freed us from all bondage, also sees us through the journey of this life unto our eternal and glorious liberty.

To even suggest that man might, through his own rebelliousness, or weakness, thwart the eternal plan of God is to debase and deny God's power and simultaneously to elevate man to a position of having power which exceeds God's. If this latter error enters the faith of man (and becomes part and parcel of the doctrine of man's salvation, as Arminianism teaches), the natural consequence is the destruction of "faith" as God has created and defined it.

True faith involves knowledge of the Word of God, holding it to be true, and a hearty trust that what God has revealed is ours (*Heidelberg Catechism* Q. 21). Faith in something that is uncertain as to its result is not true faith at all. *"Now faith is the substance of things hoped for, the evidence of things not seen." (Heb. 11:1)* "Hope," as the Bible uses that word, is not an uncertain wish, desire, or dream which might fade away. *"Blessed be the God and Father of our Lord Jesus Christ, who according to His abundant mercy has begotten us again to a living hope through the resurrection of Jesus Christ from the dead, to an inheritance incorruptible and undefiled and that does not fade away, reserved in heaven for you, who are kept by the power of God through faith for salvation ready to be revealed in the last time."* (I Pet. 1:3-5)

Hope is inseparably connected with true faith. It is God's guarantee that what we have believed will be fulfilled by God. *"For we were saved in this hope, but hope that is seen is not hope; for why does one still hope for what he sees? But if we hope for what we do not see, then we eagerly wait for it with perseverance."* (Rom. 8:24-25)

It is also reasonable that we should find this major emphasis in the Holy Scriptures, since God is not only revealing His great salvation to us, but, in performing this, He is *revealing Himself* as the author and finisher of our faith. The doctrine of the *perseverance of the saints* is essentially a doctrine which ascribes to Almighty God the authority and the ability to see His plan of salvation through to the ultimate purpose which He has intended – namely, the eternal salvation of His people. In revealing His salvation, God reveals Himself – His sovereign will, love, and grace which are the eternal attributes of God.

Let us now see what the Bible says concerning this doctrine of *the perseverance of the saints.*

Outline and Proofs from the Bible

1. Salvation is wholly *from and by God* who is able to perform all His holy will.

> Job 23:14 *"For He performs what is appointed for me, and many such things are with Him."*

> Psalm 57:1-2 *"Be merciful to me, O God, be merciful to me! For my soul trusts in You; And in the shadow of Your wings I will make my refuge, Until these calamities have passed by. I will cry out to God*

Most High, To God who performs all things for me."

Isaiah 44:23-26 *"Sing, O heavens, for the LORD has done it! Shout, you lower parts of the earth; break forth into singing, you mountains, O forest, and every tree in it! for the LORD has redeemed Jacob, and glorified Himself in Israel. Thus says the LORD, your Redeemer, and He who formed you from the womb: I am the LORD, who makes all things, Who stretches out the heavens all alone, Who spreads abroad the earth by Myself; Who frustrates the signs of the babblers, and drives diviners mad; Who turns wise men backward, and makes their knowledge foolishness; Who confirms the word of His servant, and performs the counsel of His messengers; Who says to Jerusalem, You shall be inhabited, to the cities of Judah, You shall be built, and I will raise up her waste places."*

Romans 4:20-21 *"He did not waver at the promise of God through unbelief, but was strengthened in faith, giving glory to God, and being fully convinced that what He had promised He was also able to perform."*

Philippians 1:6 *"... being confident of this very thing, that He who has begun a good work in you will complete it until the day of Jesus Christ."*

2. God is the *Creator of all*, has power over all, and is the *author and finisher of our faith*. He is willing and able to perform all His holy will.

Isaiah 43:1 *"But now, thus says the LORD, who created you, O Jacob, and He who formed you, O Israel: Fear not, for I have redeemed you; I have called you by your name; you are Mine."*

Isaiah 54:16-17 *" "Behold, I have created the blacksmith who blows the coals in the fire, who brings forth an instrument for his work; and I have created the spoiler to destroy. No weapon formed against you shall prosper, and every tongue which rises against you in judgment you shall condemn. This is the heritage of the servants of the LORD, and their righteousness is from Me," says the LORD."*

Isaiah 55:11 *"So shall My word be that goes forth from My mouth; it shall not return to Me void, but it shall accomplish what I please, and it shall prosper in the thing for which I sent it."*

Romans 8:29-31 *"For whom He foreknew, He also predestined to be conformed to the image of His Son, that He might be the firstborn among many brethren. Moreover whom He predestined, these He also called; whom He called, these He also justified; and whom He justified, these He also glorified. What then shall we say to these things? If God is for us, who can be against us?"*

Ephesians 1:11 *"... in whom also we have obtained an inheritance, being predestined according to the purpose of Him who works all things according to the counsel of His will."*

Colossians 3:3-4 *"For you died, and your life is hidden with Christ in God. When Christ who is our life appears, then you also will appear with Him in glory."*

Hebrews 7:25 *"Therefore He is also able to save to the uttermost those who come to God through Him, since He ever lives to make intercession for them."*

James 1:17-18 *"Every good gift and every perfect gift is from above, and comes down from the Father of lights, with whom there is no variation or shadow of turning. Of His own will He brought us forth by the word of truth, that we might be a kind of firstfruits of His creatures."*

3. When we read the Bible *we must read it for what it says.* When God promises us everlasting life, that means that our life is not left in doubt, but will last forever, by the power of God.

John 3:16 *"For God so loved the world that He gave His only begotten Son, that whoever believes in Him should not perish but have everlasting life."*

John 6:47 *"Most assuredly, I say to you, he who believes in Me has everlasting life."*

John 17:2 *"... as You have given Him authority over all flesh, that He should give eternal life to as many as You have given Him."*

Hebrews 9:12, 15 *"Not with the blood of goats and calves, but with His own blood He entered the Most Holy Place once for all, having obtained eternal redemption. And for this reason He is the Mediator of the new covenant, by means of death, for the redemption of the transgressions under the first covenant, that those who are called may receive the promise of the eternal inheritance."*

I John 5:11-13 *"And this is the testimony: that God has given us eternal life, and this life is in His Son. He who has the Son has life; he who does not have the Son of God does not have life. These things I have written to you who believe in the name of the Son of*

*God, that you may know that you have eternal life, and that you may
continue to believe in the name of the Son of God.*"

4. At times there are those who very much *appear as though they are
Christians,* when in fact, they are not and never were.

Matthew 7:21-23 *"Not everyone who says to Me, Lord, Lord, shall
enter the kingdom of heaven, but he who does the will of My Father
in heaven. Many will say to Me in that day, Lord, Lord, have we not
prophesied in Your name, cast out demons in Your name, and done
many wonders in Your name? And then I will declare to them, I
never knew you; depart from Me, you who practice lawlessness!*"

Matthew 15:8-9 *"These people draw near to Me with their mouth,
and honor Me with their lips, but their heart is far from Me. And in
vain they worship Me, teaching as doctrines the commandments of
men.*"

II Timothy 3:5 *"... having a form of godliness but denying its power.
And from such people turn away!*"

I John 2:19 *"They went out from us, but they were not of us; for if
they had been of us, they would have continued with us; but they
went out that they might be made manifest, that none of them were
of us.*"

5. While man is commanded to believe and remain faithful, *the ground
for the assurance* of our salvation rests on the *faithfulness of God* to
keep His promise to us.

Psalm 89:1-2, 5, 8, 24 *"I will sing of the mercies of the LORD
forever; With my mouth will I make known Your faithfulness to all
generations. For I have said, Mercy shall be built up forever; Your
faithfulness You shall establish in the very heavens. And the heavens
will praise Your wonders, O LORD; Your faithfulness also in the
congregation of the saints. O LORD God of hosts, Who is mighty
like You, O LORD? Your faithfulness also surrounds You. But My
faithfulness and My mercy shall be with him, And in My name his
horn shall be exalted.*"

Isaiah 54:10 *"For the mountains shall depart and the hills be
removed, but My kindness shall not depart from you, nor shall My
covenant of peace be removed, says the LORD, who has mercy on
you.*"

I Corinthians 1:7-9 *"... so that you come short in no gift, eagerly waiting for the revelation of our Lord Jesus Christ, who will also confirm you to the end, that you may be blameless in the day of our Lord Jesus Christ. God is faithful, by whom you were called into the fellowship of His Son, Jesus Christ our Lord."*

I Corinthians 10:13 *"No temptation has overtaken you except such as is common to man; but God is faithful, who will not allow you to be tempted beyond what you are able, but with the temptation will also make the way of escape, that you may be able to bear it."*

I Thessalonians 5:23-24 *"Now may the God of peace Himself sanctify you completely; and may your whole spirit, soul, and body be preserved blameless at the coming of our Lord Jesus Christ. He who calls you is faithful, who also will do it."*

II Timothy 2:13 *"If we are faithless, He remains faithful; He cannot deny Himself."*

Hebrews 10:23 *"Let us hold fast the confession of our hope without wavering, for He who promised is faithful."*

I John 1:9 *"If we confess our sins, He is faithful and just to forgive us our sins and to cleanse us from all unrighteousness."*

6. It is *God who preserves His elect in the faith* which He Himself has given to them.

Psalm 37:28 *"For the LORD loves justice, And does not forsake His saints; They are preserved forever, But the descendants of the wicked shall be cut off."*

John 6:37, 39-40 *"All that the Father gives Me will come to Me, and the one who comes to Me I will by no means cast out. This is the will of the Father who sent Me, that of all He has given Me I should lose nothing, but should raise it up at the last day. And this is the will of Him who sent Me, that everyone who sees the Son and believes in Him may have everlasting life; and I will raise him up at the last day."*

John 17:11-12, 15 *"Now I am no longer in the world, but these are in the world, and I come to You. Holy Father, keep through Your name those whom You have given Me, that they may be one as We are. While I was with them in the world, I kept them in Your name. Those whom You gave Me I have kept; and none of them is lost except the son of perdition, that the Scripture might be fulfilled. I do not pray that You should take them out of the world, but that You should keep them from the evil one."*

Romans 8:33, 35-39 *"Who shall bring a charge against God's elect? It is God who justifies. Who shall separate us from the love of Christ? Shall tribulation, or distress, or persecution, or famine, or nakedness, or peril, or sword? As it is written: For Your sake we are killed all day long; we are accounted as sheep for the slaughter. Yet in all these things we are more than conquerors through Him who loved us. For I am persuaded that neither death nor life, nor angels nor principalities nor powers, nor things present nor things to come, nor height nor depth, nor any other created thing, shall be able to separate us from the love of God which is in Christ Jesus our Lord."*

II Corinthians 4:14 *"... knowing that He who raised up the Lord Jesus will also raise us up with Jesus, and will present us with you."*

Ephesians 1:5, 13-14 *"... having predestined us to adoption as sons by Jesus Christ to Himself, according to the good pleasure of His will, in Him you also trusted, after you heard the word of truth, the gospel of your salvation; in whom also, having believed, you were sealed with the Holy Spirit of promise, who is the guarantee of our inheritance until the redemption of the purchased possession, to the praise of His glory."*

Philippians 1:6 *"... being confident of this very thing, that He who has begun a good work in you will complete it until the day of Jesus Christ."*

II Timothy 4:18 *"And the Lord will deliver me from every evil work and preserve me for His heavenly kingdom. To Him be glory forever and ever. Amen!"*

Hebrews 10:14 *"For by one offering He has perfected forever those who are being sanctified."*

I John 5:20 *"And we know that the Son of God has come and has given us an understanding, that we may know Him who is true; and we are in Him who is true, in His Son Jesus Christ. This is the true God and eternal life."*

Jude v. 1 *"Jude, a servant of Jesus Christ, and brother of James, To those who are called, sanctified by God the Father, and preserved in Jesus Christ."*

Jude vv. 24-25 *"Now to Him who is able to keep you from stumbling, and to present you faultless before the presence of His glory with exceeding joy, to God our Savior, who alone is wise, be glory and majesty, dominion and power, both now and forever. Amen."*

7. Because *God preserves* us by grace in the faith, *we persevere* in the faith.

Ephesians 2:10 *"For we are His workmanship, created in Christ Jesus for good works, which God prepared beforehand that we should walk in them."*

Philippians 2:12-13 *"Therefore, my beloved, as you have always obeyed, not as in my presence only, but now much more in my absence, work out your own salvation with fear and trembling; for it is God who works in you both to will and to do for His good pleasure."*

I Peter 1:3-5 *"Blessed be the God and Father of our Lord Jesus Christ, who according to His abundant mercy has begotten us again to a living hope through the resurrection of Jesus Christ from the dead, to an inheritance incorruptible and undefiled and that does not fade away, reserved in heaven for you, who are kept by the power of God through faith for salvation ready to be revealed in the last time."*

Jude vv. 20-21 *"But you, beloved, building yourselves up on your most holy faith, praying in the Holy Spirit, keep yourselves in the love of God, looking for the mercy of our Lord Jesus Christ unto eternal life."*

8. It is God who comforts us with *the assurance* that our salvation is always *secure in His hand.*

Jeremiah 32:38-41 *"They shall be My people, and I will be their God; then I will give them one heart and one way, that they may fear Me forever, for the good of them and their children after them. And I will make an everlasting covenant with them, that I will not turn away from doing them good; but I will put My fear in their hearts so that they will not depart from Me. Yes, I will rejoice over them to do them good, and I will assuredly plant them in this land, with all My heart and with all My soul."*

John 5:24 *""Most assuredly, I say to you, he who hears My word and believes in Him who sent Me has everlasting life, and shall not come into judgment, but has passed from death into life."*

John 6:39 *"This is the will of the Father who sent Me, that of all He has given Me I should lose nothing, but should raise it up at the last day."*

John 10:27-30 *"My sheep hear My voice, and I know them, and they follow Me. And I give them eternal life, and they shall never perish; neither shall anyone snatch them out of My hand. My Father, who has given them to Me, is greater than all; and no one is able to snatch them out of My Father's hand. I and My Father are one."*

Romans 8:1 *"There is therefore now no condemnation to those who are in Christ Jesus, who do not walk according to the flesh, but according to the Spirit."*

Ephesians 4:30 *"And do not grieve the Holy Spirit of God, by whom you were sealed for the day of redemption."*

II Timothy 1:12 *"For this reason I also suffer these things; nevertheless I am not ashamed, for I know whom I have believed and am persuaded that He is able to keep what I have committed to Him until that Day."*

Hebrews 12:28 *"Therefore, since we are receiving a kingdom which cannot be shaken, let us have grace, by which we may serve God acceptably with reverence and godly fear."*

I John 2:25 *"And this is the promise that He has promised us – eternal life."*

The Bible is replete with the assurances that what God has begun He is willing and able to finish. These are only a few of the many references to this work of God. If we rightly see that God (not man) is the one who has begun the work of salvation and worked faith in us, then He (not man) will be able to complete it. This is the very nature of God who reveals Himself to us in his Word.

QUESTIONS

1. Why is it important to believe that God is the Creator in connection with this doctrine of the perseverance of the saints?

2. What is meant when we say that the Bible is not just a revelation of God's plan, but a revelation of God? How are they connected?

3. According to Ephesians 2:10, how can we see that the whole plan of God in His salvation was that we should persevere in faith and in

good works?

4. What two passages of the Scripture would you select which most clearly teach this doctrine of the perseverance of the saints?

5. Why is this doctrine not only biblical, but logical?

6. Why is it true that this doctrine of security in God's grace and power does not make us careless about either our faith or our life?

Conclusion

I t is not the intent of this study to attack and weaken the faith of those who may hold to Arminian doctrines. On the contrary, my purpose is simply to teach what the Scriptures say on this most important matter of salvation, and if necessary, to correct false and inconsistent beliefs. I hope the result will be a greater gratitude to God for His saving grace – *"for of Him and through Him and to Him are all things, to whom be glory forever. Amen."* (Rom. 11:36)

When we say that Arminian doctrines are a "works" religion, we are not saying that they hold to a "works righteousness" as such, even though they may come perilously close. The theology of Arminianism does rest on a "work" of man throughout to attain and maintain his salvation. This makes God dependant on man to carry out His plan.

Arminianism has attempted to do the impossible – to say that *salvation is by grace* through faith in Christ, and at the same time, to say that it is *not totally by grace*. In this it is a failure, for grace is not able to be mixed with works and still remain grace. Therefore, I would hope that anyone caught up in this theology would carefully consider again the consistent truths of Scripture presented in this study.

My primary purpose is to address those whose heritage is in the Reformed faith and who may have doubts or misunderstandings about these doctrines. In some circles today these doctrines are not even taught any longer, and we see the sons and daughters of the Reformed heritage drift off into theological positions and churches whose teachings do not recognize a sovereign God. This is dishonoring to Him.

I hope that this study is more than just a theological exercise, but makes your faith come alive with greater comfort for your souls and thanksgiving in your lives to God.

My greatest desire is that our covenant children understand these truths and will teach them to their children so that it may be said that the *faith of our fathers is living still*, in the hearts and lives of generations to come.

SOLI DEO GLORIA

Appendix

- Summary of the Canons of Dort

- The Remonstrance

- Hymn: *"By Grace Alone"*

- Bibliography and Suggested Reading

A Summary of the
The Canons of Dort

This summary is written to facilitate a quick reference for the study of the various doctrines contained in the *Canons of Dort*. It should not be considered a substitute for reading the Canons themselves, but may serve as a quick overview. I have tried to reduce each Article of the Canons to a single, central point. The order of these "Heads of Doctrine" follows the original Canons and are not in the order of *TULIP* as we often study them.

Likewise the Rejection of Errors in the Canons should be studied to see how many of the objections raised are very much like those we hear today.

FIRST HEAD OF DOCTRINE

Divine Election and Reprobation

(Unconditional Election)

1. God would be just to leave all men in their sin and condemn all men.

2. God shows His sovereign love in the sending of Jesus Christ.

3. In mercy, God sends ministers to preach the gospel to all men.

4. Unbelievers perish in their sins while believers of the gospel are saved.

5. God is not guilty for man's sin; God is the Author, not of sin, but of faith and salvation.

6. God eternally decreed before the foundation of the world who is elected (chosen) for salvation and who shall perish in their sin.

7. Election is defined as a gracious, sovereign act of God by which He chooses a certain number of persons to redemption in Christ.

8. God's election is one – both in the Old and New Testaments.

9. Election is not founded on any good conditions which man may later demonstrate and which God is able to foresee.

10. Election is by the good pleasure of God's perfect will.

11. God's election is unalterable.

12. The fruits of faith eventually give assurance of one's election.

13. Assurance of election does not make believers careless or callous, but humble and faithful in their service of love and thanksgiving.

14. The doctrine of election was preached in both the Old and New Testaments and should be taught in the Church of God today.

15. Those not elected by God are passed by in God's eternal decree (the decree of Reprobation), and are left to continue in their sin unto condemnation.

16. Those who continue to use the means of grace, yet do not have an assured confidence regarding of soul should not be alarmed, nor doubt their election, nor fear that they might be reprobate. Those who persevere in the faith prove their election, while those who cast off the faith prove their reprobation.

17. Believers ought not to doubt the election and salvation of their children, who are members of the Covenant of Grace.

18. The Scriptures teach us that it is dishonoring to God to doubt that He has the right to show grace to the elect and condemn the reprobate.

REJECTION OF ERRORS

with regard to the Doctrine of Election

The Synod rejects...

1. the error of having election based upon foreseen faith and perseverance in faith by man.

2. the error of saying that there are two kinds of election – one more general which brings men to faith (who later could be lost), and another more definite election which results in salvation.

3. the error that faith is a condition to salvation.

4. the error which says that election depends on how men use the light of nature, or makes it dependent on pious living.

5. the error which says that complete and decisive election depends upon foreseen perseverance in faith (*ie.* man's perseverance is a condition for God's election).

6. the error that those elected may still perish.

7. the error that the elect may never be certain of their election.

8. the error that God did not pass by any men and thus leave them in their state of condemnation.

9. the error that certain nations are better than others and therefore God shows grace to them and excludes others.

THE SECOND HEAD OF DOCTRINE

The Death of Christ, and the Redemption of Man Thereby

(Limited Atonement)

1. God's justice requires that all sin, since it is against His high majesty, must be punished with everlasting punishment of body and soul.

2. Since we could not satisfy God's perfect justice by ourselves, He sent His Son to make full satisfaction in man's place.

3. Christ's death is the only satisfaction for sin – sufficient to cleanse the whole world of sin.

4. Christ's death was perfect because He was truly God and truly man.

5. The gospel of Christ must be preached to all men.

6. Those who reject the gospel do so because of their sin and not because the work of Christ was insufficient.

7. Believers have faith solely by the grace of God given to them from eternity – not by their own merit.

8. God's purpose in Jesus Christ is to make the death of Christ efficient (effectual) in the saving of His elect only.

9. This purpose of God continues to be accomplished, regardless of all opposition, for the gathering of the Church which will always exist with Christ as the foundation. This Church will praise God both in time and eternity.

REJECTION OF ERRORS

with regard to Limited Atonement

The Synod rejects...

1. the error of those who say that Christ did not die to save anyone in particular, and hold to the possibility that Christ's death would be perfect even if no one believed.

2. the error of those who deny that God confirmed the new covenant of grace through the blood of Jesus.

3. the error of those who say that Christ's satisfaction did not merit salvation itself, but only allowed the Father to make new conditions which depend upon man's free will.

4. the error that says that Christ's death allowed God to remove the demand for a perfect obedience in faith, but allows imperfect faith to be considered as a perfect obedience to the law.

5. the error of those who say that no one is worthy of condemnation due to original sin, because all men are in the covenant of grace.

6. the error that man's free will may combine with God's grace to bring about salvation.

7. the error that says Christ did not die for the elect, since they do not

need the death of Christ.

THE THIRD AND FOURTH HEADS OF DOCTRINE

The Corruption of Man, His Conversion to God,

and the Manner Thereof

(Total Depravity and Irresistible Grace)

1. Man was created perfectly in the image of God, but the fall into sin totally involved him in all that is contrary to perfection.

2. All of Adam's posterity are corrupt by nature, Christ excepted.

3. All men are conceived and born in sin and without the Holy Spirit are neither willing nor able to return to God.

4. Man still has a knowledge of God in natural things, but it cannot bring him to a saving knowledge of God and he cannot use it properly even in things natural and civil. In the end, this "light" proclaims man guilty and leaves him inexcusable before God.

5. The law reveals man's sin, but cannot save him.

6. Nature and the law do not save, but God saves in the Old and New Testaments by the operation of the Holy Spirit through the preaching of the gospel.

7. By the sovereign good pleasure of God, salvation is revealed to many who are to respond with humble and grateful hearts.

8. The gospel is to be preached to all men sincerely.

9. Because of sin within man, they reject the gospel or allow other cares and pleasures to choke it out. This is not the fault of the gospel.

10. Those who believe the gospel do so, not by their fallen free wills, but by the effectual call of God.

11. The Holy Spirit effectually regenerates the heart, gives new qualities to the will, brings the dead heart to life, and gives the gift of faith to God's elect.

12. Repentance and faith are supernatural works of God the Holy Spirit in man, whereby the will of man is activated and enabled to repent and believe.

13. This working of God in man is a wondrous mystery, yet man believes it by the grace of God.

14. Faith is the gift of God – infused, inbreathed into man. God produces both the will to believe and the act of believing.

15. God owes salvation to nobody. The believer, therefore, owes eternal gratitude to God and must pray to God for others who remain in unbelief.

16. Regeneration by the Holy Spirit does not take away the will of man so that he becomes just a "senseless stock and block", but it renews the will of man, enabling him to make a responsible confession of faith.

17. The gift of faith from God does not exclude, but includes the continued use of the means of grace – the admonitions of the gospel, the influence (preaching and study) of the Word, the sacraments, and church discipline. God uses these means to bring us to faith, and we must continue in them.

REJECTION OF ERRORS

With Regard to Total Depravity and

Irresistible Grace

The Synod rejects...

1. the error that teaches that original sin does not condemn all men.

2. the error that says that man did not possess goodness, righteousness, and holiness as a part of his will before the Fall, and that, therefore, these were not lost from the will of man after the Fall.

3. the error of those who say that the will of man was not affected by the Fall.

4. the error that says that man is not totally dead in sin, but can still turn to God under his own power.

5. the error that man can gradually move from the common grace of God to the saving grace of God by himself.

6. the error of those who say that man's will after conversion is essentially no different, and therefore, faith is not a gift of God but an act of man (except in the power given by God to attain it).

7. the error of those who say that the grace of God in our conversion is only advisory – directing us, rather than performing a real work within us.

8. the error of those who say that man may resist God and the Holy Spirit in the matter of regeneration.

9. the error that says that grace and free will of man initiate conversion, and that God does not begin to work in man until man in his free will moves first.

THE FIFTH HEAD OF DOCTRINE

The Perseverance of the Saints

1. Those whom God has called into Christ, and regenerated, he also delivers from the dominion of sin, while in this life there remain the infirmities of the flesh.

2. The weakness of the flesh and daily sin causes even the best works of the saints to be blemished with sin in order to humble men and drive them to Christ for refuge. The result must be mortification of the flesh, piety, and a striving for the goal of perfection which will be reached after this life.

3. Believers, because of this indwelling sin, could not remain faithful if left to themselves. It is God who is faithful to mercifully confirm and powerfully to preserve the saints, even to the end.

4. Man in the weakness of his flesh must be watchful and prayerful that he will not reject the influence that God exerts in his life, and

thereby fall into great sin. Although the saints backslide, they are not ultimately lost (*cf.* David and Peter).

5. When the saints fall into grave sin, their faith is weakened and they lose their sense of God's favor until they repent and turn to God again.

6. God does not change His purpose of election and allow sinners to utterly fall away by withdrawing His Holy Spirit, thus allowing them to fall into everlasting destruction.

7. God does not remove the seed of regeneration (the Holy Spirit), and by His Word and Holy Spirit works repentance in the hearts of those He has elected that they might return humbly unto Him in faith.

8. It is not by the merits or strength of man, but by the free mercy of God that man does not totally fall away from God and perish. Man, left to himself would surely perish eternally, but God never deserts His chosen ones nor revokes His eternal purpose.

9. Believers do obtain the assurance of faith which says that they will forever be members of the Church, have forgiveness of sins, and everlasting life.

10. Assurance of salvation comes from faith in the promises of the gospel, which are worked in us by the Word and the Spirit of God, and from a holy desire to preserve a good conscience and perform good works.

11. Believers struggle with various carnal doubts and do not always feel the full force of this assurance, but God will never tempt them above their ability to bear it, but makes for them a way of escape; also the Holy Spirit works assurance in us.

12. This doctrine of perseverance (that the saints may never be lost) does not work pride in man, but works humility, reverence, piety, patience, prayer, endurance in suffering, confession of the truth, and rejoicing.

13. Those who are recovered from backsliding are not filled with pride, but take greater care lest they be allowed to fall into more grievous torment and God turn His face from them again.

14. What work God has begun by the preaching of the gospel, He will perfect by the hearing and reading of the Word, by meditations, teachings, warnings, by promises of the Word, and by the holy sacraments.

15. The carnal (unconverted) mind is not able to comprehend this doctrine, and thus mock and ridicule it, but the saints of God take great comfort in it.

REJECTION OF ERRORS

with regard to the Perseverance of the Saints

The Synod rejects...

1. the error that says perseverance is not the fruit of election, but a condition of the New Covenant which man must fulfill by his own free will.

2. the error of those who say that God gives man the power to persevere, but that man has the free will to accept or deny this power of God.

3. the error that teaches that man can and often does fall from justifying faith and from grace and salvation.

4. the error that says that true believers can commit the unforgivable sin against the Holy Spirit and hence be lost eternally.

5. the error that says that without further revelation of God we have no certainty of our perseverance in faith.

6. the error that says that this doctrine of perseverance causes men to live lives of low morals and prayerlessness.

7. the error that says that a temporary faith (not a true, saving faith) is the same as true faith for as long as it exists.

8. the error that says that a person could be regenerated more than once.

9. the error that claims that Christ nowhere prayed that believers

should continue in faith.

FROM THE CONCLUDING STATEMENT
OF THE CANONS OF DORT

"The doctrine of this creed is drawn from the Word of God and is in harmony with other Reformed creeds of the day. The Synod rejects the notion that the doctrine of God's sovereign grace set forth in the creed gives cause for men to sin or have a false sense of assurance. Likewise it does not make God either arbitrary or the author of sin. To the enemies of the Reformed churches, a warning is issued not to misrepresent these teachings. Adherents to the creed are likewise exhorted to further these teachings, and warned to take care that these doctrines are taught within the limits herein set forth, that the piety and holiness of Christian lives may bring glory to God."

"May Jesus Christ, the son of God, who, seated at the Father's right hand, gives gifts to men, sanctify us in the truth; bring to the truth those who err; shut the mouths of the calumniators of sound doctrine, and endue the faithful ministers of his Word with the spirit of wisdom and discretion, that all their discourses may tend to the glory of God, and the edification of those who hear them. Amen."

(final words of the "Conclusion")

The Remonstrance

I thought that it might be well to include the statements of the Remonstrants for study. They are rather brief and include two parts: first, a rejection of basic Calvinism and secondly, the five positive articles of their own teaching. This Remonstrance was formulated in 1610 and was the cause for the meeting of the Synod of Dort.

It is clear that they misrepresent and/or misunderstand both the teachings of Calvinism and the teachings of the Bible. Modern Arminianism has gone even farther than these statements of 1610.

The text for this Remonstrance is taken from *The Creeds of Christendom* by Philip Schaff, Vol. I, pp. 517-519 and from the same work, Vol. III, pp. 545-549. The comments, regarding the Remonstrance, made by Philip Schaff are included below in (italics).

THE DOCTRINES REJECTED BY REMONSTRANTS ARE THUS STATED:

"1. That God has, before the fall, and even before the creation of man, by an unchangeable decree, foreordained some to eternal life and others to eternal damnation, without any regard to righteousness or sin, to obedience or disobedience, and simply because it so pleased him, in order to show the glory of his righteousness to the one class and his mercy to the other. *(This is the supralapsarian view.)*

2. That God, in view of the fall, and in just condemnation of our first parents and their posterity, ordained to exempt a part of mankind from the consequences of the fall, and to save them by his

free grace, but to leave the rest, without regard to age or moral condition, to their condemnation, for the glory of his righteousness. *(The sublapsarian view.)*

3. That Christ died, not for all men, but only for the elect.

4. That the Holy Spirit works in the elect by irresistible grace, so that they *must* be converted and be saved; while the grace necessary and sufficient for conversion, faith, and salvation is withheld from the rest, although they are externally called and invited by the revealed will of God.

5. That those who have received this irresistible grace can never totally and finally lose it, but are guided and preserved by the same grace to the end.

These doctrines, the Remonstrants declare, and are not contained in the Word of God nor in the Heidelberg Catechism, and are unedifying, yea dangerous, and should not be preached to Christian people."

THE FOLLOWING ARTICLES CONTAIN THE TEACHINGS OF THE REMONSTRANTS:

ARTICLE I

That God, by an eternal, unchangeable purpose in Jesus Christ his Son, before the foundation of the world, hath determined, out of the fallen, sinful race of men, to save in Christ, for Christ's sake, and through Christ, those who, through the grace of the Holy Ghost, shall believe on this his Son Jesus, and shall persevere in this faith and obedience of faith, through this grace, even to the end; and, on the other hand, to leave the incorrigible and unbelieving in sin and under wrath, and to condemn them as alienated from Christ, according to the word of the gospel of John 3:36: "He that believeth on the Son hath everlasting life: and he that believeth not the Son shall not see life; but the wrath of God abideth on him," and according to other passages of Scripture also.

(Election and condemnation are thus conditioned by fore-knowledge, and made dependent on the foreseen faith or unbelief of men.)

ARTICLE II

That, agreeably thereto, Jesus Christ, the Saviour of the world, died for all men and for every man, so that he has obtained for them all, by his death on the cross, redemption and the forgiveness of sins; yet that no one actually enjoys this forgiveness of sins except the believer, according to the word of the gospel of John 3:16: "God so loved the world that he gave his only-begotten Son, that whosoever believeth in him should not perish, but have everlasting life." And in the First Epistle of John 2:2: "And he is the propitiation for our sins; and not for ours only, but also for the sins of the whole world."

(The Arminians agree with the orthodox in holding the doctrine of a vicarious or expiatory atonement, in opposition to the Socinians; but they soften it down, and represent its direct effect to be to enable God, consistently with his justice and veracity, to enter into a new covenant with men, under which pardon is conveyed to all men on condition of repentance and faith. The immediate effect of Christ's death was not the salvation, but only the salvability of sinners by the removal of the legal obstacles, and opening the door for pardon and reconciliation. They reject the doctrine of a limited atonement, which is connected with the supralapsarian view of predestination, but is disowned by moderate Calvinists, who differ from the Arminians in all other points. Calvin himself says that Christ died "sufficienter pro omnibus, efficaciter pro electis". ("sufficient for all, efficacious for the elect" - translation mine)

ARTICLE III

That man has not saving grace of himself, nor of the energy of his free will, inasmuch as he, in the state of apostasy and sin, can of and by himself neither think, will, nor do anything that is truly good (such as saving Faith eminently is); but that it is needful that he be born again of God in Christ, through his Holy Spirit, and renewed in understanding, inclination, or will, and all his powers, in order that he may rightly understand, think, will, and effect what is truly good, according to the Word of Christ, John 15:5: "Without me ye can do nothing."

ARTICLE IV

That this grace of God is the beginning, continuance, and accomplishment of all good, even to this extent, that the regenerate man himself, without prevenient or assisting, awakening, following and co-operative grace, can neither think, will, nor do good, nor withstand any temptations to evil; so that all good deeds or movements, that can be conceived, must be ascribed to the grace of God in Christ. But as respects the mode of the operation of this grace, it is not irresistible, inasmuch as it is written concerning many, that they have resisted the Holy Ghost. Acts 7, and elsewhere in many places.

ARTICLE V

That those who are incorporated into Christ by a true faith, and have thereby become partakers of his life-giving Spirit, have thereby full power to strive against Satan, sin, the world, and their own flesh, and to win the victory; it being well understood that it is ever through the assisting grace of the Holy Ghost; and that Jesus Christ assists them through his Spirit in all temptations, extends to them his hand, and if only they are ready for the conflict, and desire his help, and are not inactive, keeps them from falling, so that they, by no craft or power of Satan, can be misled or plucked out of Christ's hands, according to the Word of Christ, John 10:28: "Neither shall any man pluck them out of my hand." But whether they are capable, through negligence, of forsaking again the first beginnings of their life in Christ, of again returning to this present evil world, of turning away from the holy doctrine which was delivered them, of losing a good conscience, of becoming devoid of grace, that must be more particularly determined out of the Holy Scripture, before we ourselves can teach it with full persuasion of our minds.

(On this point the disciples of Arminius went further, and taught the possibility of a total and final fall of believers from grace. They appealed to such passages as Solomon and Judas. They moreover denied, with the Roman Catholics, that anybody can have a certainty of salvation except by special revelation.)

———————

These Articles, thus set forth and taught, the Remonstrants deem agreeable to the Word of God, tending to edification, and as regards this argument, sufficient for salvation, so that it is not necessary or edifying to rise higher or to descend deeper.

By Grace Alone

Paul H. Treick, 1987   Tune: Melita

You are our God, and we your race,
elected by your sovereign grace.
Not by the works which we have done
but by the cross the victory's won.
O keep this truth within our heart
that from it we may ne'er depart.

By nature we depraved did dwell
under your curse, deserving hell;
sinful, corrupt in every part,
not one pure motive in our heart.
Had you not looked on us in grace
we would remain a perished race.

In love eternal; you did choose
to save your sheep, their bonds to loose.
No good did we within us have
to claim your gracious plan to save.
Elected by your grace alone,
holy to stand before your throne!

Incarnate did your Son appear,
a sacrifice, a lamb most pure,
to make atonement for his sheep
and perfectly your will to keep.
Now cleansed from sin, and righteous, we
are sons and heirs eternally.

The blood of Christ by grace supplied
was by your Spirit's power applied.
Your Spirit we could not resist
who breathed new life into our breast.
Our souls alive which once were dead
sing praise to Christ, the Lord, our Head.

With all your saints we are preserved
to enter heav'n, a place reserved.
Secure we're kept within your care
lest we be lost to Satan's snare.
O sovereign God, our praise we raise
for our salvation, full and free.

This hymn of thanks, O Lord, we bring,
for by your grace alone we sing.
Employ our lives in every sphere
your law to keep, your Name to fear.
'By grace alone' – this doctrine pure –
our only comfort does secure.

Amen.

This hymn was written as a confession of the doctrine of God's sovereign grace. The first stanza is an introduction and the last a conclusion. Stanza's two through six contain the basic teachings of the Five Points of Calvinism: Total Depravity, Unconditional Election, Limited Atonement, Irresistible Grace, and the Perseverance of the Saints.

This hymn may be sung to the tune of "Melita," commonly known as "Eternal Father, strong to save..."

Bibliography
And Suggested Reading

Boettner, Loraine. *The Reformed Doctrine of Predestination*. Philadelphia, PA: Presbyterian and Reformed Publishing Co., 1966.

Girod, Gordon. *The Deeper Faith*. Grand Rapids, Michigan: Baker Book House, 1978.

Klooster, Fred. *Calvin's Doctrine of Predestination*. Grand Rapids, Michigan: Baker Book House, 1977.

Kuiper, R. B. *The Bible Tells Us So*. London: The Banner of Truth Trust, 1968.

Kuiper, R. B. *For Whom Did Christ Die?*. Grand Rapids, Michigan: Baker Book House, 1959.

Luther, Martin. *The Bondage of the Will*. Fleming H. Revell Company, 1957.

Murray, John. *The Sovereignty of God*. Philadelphia: Great Commissions Publications, 1965.

Murray, John. *The Atonement*. Philadelphia, PA: Presbyterian and Reformed Publishing Co., 1962.

Murray, John. *Calvin on Scripture and Divine Sovereignty*. Grand Rapids, Michigan: Baker Book House, 1960.

Murray, John. *The Imputation of Adam's Sin*. Nutley, New Jersey: Presbyterian and Reformed Publishing Co. 1977.

Murray, John. *Redemption Accomplished and Applied*. London: Banner of Truth Trust, 1961.

Ness, Christopher. *An Antidote Against Arminianism*. Edmonton, AB., Canada: Still Waters Revival Books, 1988.

Owen, John. *A Display of Arminianism*. Edmonton, AB., Canada: Still Waters Revival Books, 1989.

Palmer, Edwin. *The Five Points of Calvinism*. Grand Rapids, Michigan: Baker Book House, 1972.

Petersen, Henry. *The Canons of Dort, A Study Guide.* Grand Rapids, Michigan: Baker Book House, 1968.

Pink, Arthur. *The Sovereignty of God.* Grand Rapids, Michigan: Baker Book House, 1930.

Schaff, Philip. *The Creeds of Christendom.* Volumes I & III.   New York: Harper & Brothers, Franklin Square, 1881.

Spencer, Duane Edward. *TULIP The Five Points of Calvinism in the Light of Scripture.* Grand Rapids, Michigan: Baker Book House, 1979.

Steele, David N. and Thomas, Curtis C. *The Five Points of Calvinism Defined, Defended, Documented.* Philadelphia, PA: Presbyterian and Reformed Publishing Co., 1965.

Talbot, Kenneth G. & Crampton, W. Gary. *Calvinism, Hyper-Calvinism & Arminianism.* Lakeland, Florida: Whitefield Publications, 1990.

The Three Forms of Unity. Published by the Reformed Church in the United States, 2006.

Van Til, Cornelius. *The Sovereignty of Grace.* Philadelphia, PA: Presbyterian and Reformed Publishing Co., 1969.

Warfield, Benjamin B. *The Plan of Salvation.* Grand Rapids, Michigan: Wm. B. Eerdmans Publishing Co., 1966.

Winter, Ernst F. Editor. *Luther - Erasmus Discourse on Free Will.* New York: Frederick Ungar Publishing Co., Inc., 1961.

Made in the USA
Coppell, TX
22 September 2020